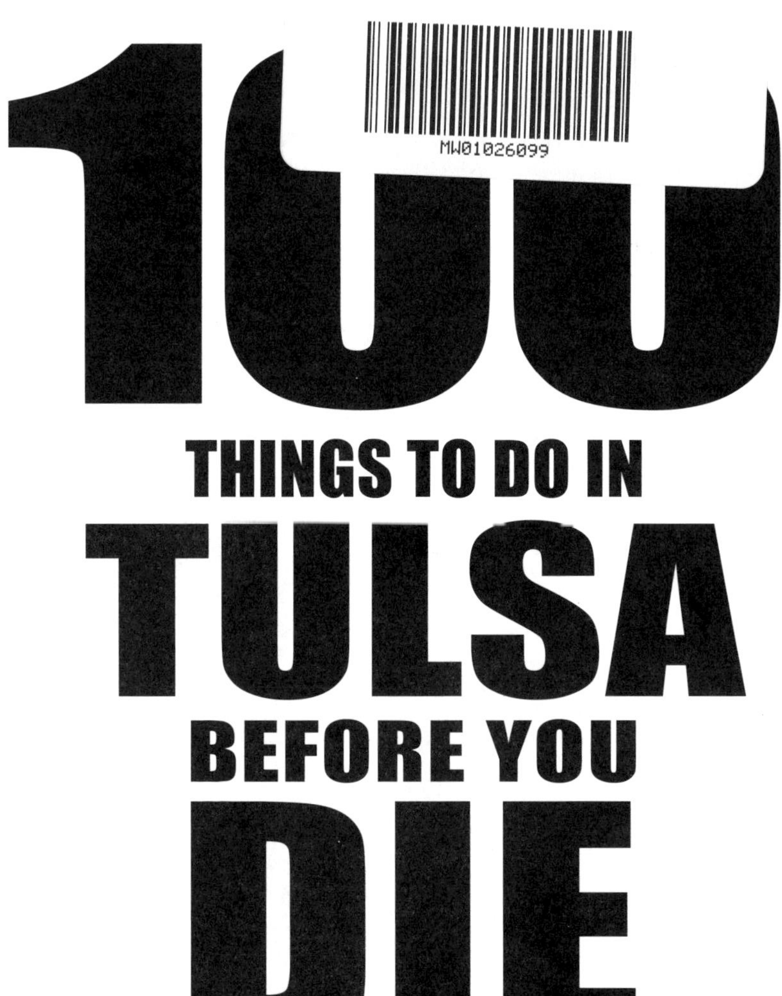
MW01026099
100
THINGS TO DO IN
TULSA
BEFORE YOU
DIE

100 THINGS TO DO IN TULSA BEFORE YOU DIE

TERI FRENCH

Reedy Press
PO Box 5131
St. Louis, MO 63139, USA
www.reedypress.com

Library of Congress Control Number: 2019952609

ISBN: 9781681062518

Design by Jill Halpin

Printed in the United States of America
20 21 22 23 24   5 4 3 2 1

DEDICATION

This book is dedicated to my mom, Sandi, and my granddaughter, Aviah.

HARDWARE
STOVES – RANGES
REFRIGERATORS
THE

CONTENTS

Music and Entertainment

Sports and Recreation

Culture and History

Shopping and Fashion

PREFACE

The beautiful city of Tulsa, Oklahoma is home to 400,000 people. It's a big city with a small-town feel, a very tight community, and a large variety of culture, history, and tradition.

Tulsa has so much to offer local artists and entrepreneurs. The city is full of possibilities and many young professionals have taken advantage of them. On nearly every corner you will find quaint independent bookstores, gift shops, coffee shops, and studios. All are places where ideas or dreams have become realities for many small business owners.

Consequently, coming up with only one hundred things to do and see in this amazing city was quite challenging. There are many different things to experience here and the most special part of it all is that many of them were created by local Tulsans.

As a "transplanted Tulsan," originally born and raised back east, I was brought to Tulsa at the tender age of fifteen when my mother remarried. Although I did not know a soul here, I quickly made friends, and now that I have spent more than half of my life in Tulsa, I feel that I am officially entitled to call myself an Okie and a Tulsan. Having lived here for over thirty years, I have discovered some quirky, fun, and special places in this city that many lifelong Tulsans may not even know about, and am excited to share them with you in this book.

In the last thirty-four years I have seen areas that were once open fields become bustling shopping centers, hospitals, and strip malls. I have watched desolate, skid-row downtown Tulsa turn itself into a thriving, busy metropolis suitable for local artists and people with vision.

When I was sixteen and got my first car, my best friend Kim and I wanted to explore downtown. We loved the tall, ornate, art deco buildings, but back in the '80s, there was no Arts District, Pearl District, or Blue Dome as we know it today. My friend and I got lost on the many one-way streets, and the dark, empty buildings made it quite a harrowing experience. Now those once-lonely buildings have had new life breathed into them. Major revitalization projects have those buildings housing breweries, small shops, and cafés where you can get the most unique and amazing things.

I hope in sharing some of these places with you, you will visit them time and time again to help small business owners keep thriving in this wonderful community.

ACKNOWLEDGMENTS

I would like to personally thank the over three thousand Facebook friends who assisted me with some of the places mentioned in this book. So many of you love Tulsa as much as I do, and your thoughts, opinions, and help were monumental. I truly appreciate your support, following, and encouragement.

Thank you to my close friends and family for your unwavering support and encouragement. Your cheers from the sidelines gave me the courage to do this with confidence.

This was such a fun writing project. A special thank you goes to the people at Reedy Press for this opportunity. I love the city of Tulsa and appreciate the confidence they placed in me to see this through.

VALKYRIE
SERIOUS DRINKS
THE
EMERALD
GALLERY

FOOD AND DRINK

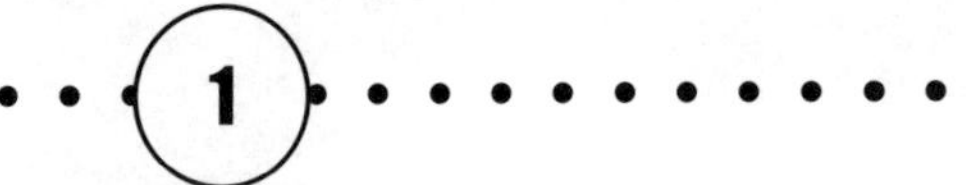

GET IN
ON HOP JAM

Three of the famous musicians that call Tulsa home are the adorable Hanson brothers. After more than twenty years in the music business, the brothers Isaac, Taylor, and Zac started their own label of beer and formed Hanson Brothers Beer Company in 2013.

The launch of this new brand inspired the brothers to start the Hop Jam Beer and Music Festival the following year, and it has become one of the largest craft beer and music festivals in the United States today.

The festival usually takes place on the third Sunday in May. Musicians and breweries from all over the world converge in Tulsa, Oklahoma for this one-day festival packed with music and good craft beer.

Every year national recording artists and award-winning breweries are brought in, the streets in the downtown Tulsa Arts District are closed down, and thousands of people gather to enjoy a variety of craft beer, music, and culture.

Hop Jam Beer & Music Festival—Tulsa Arts District
Third weekend in May

www.instagram.com/thehopjam
www.twitter.com/thehopjam
www.facebook.com/thehopjam

2

ENJOY A DEEP-FRIED DAY
AT THE TULSA STATE FAIR

Once a year, the fair rolls in and it's the city's largest family-friendly event. It occurs just after Labor Day in September and runs for eleven consecutive days. Located at the Expo Square Fairgrounds at 21st Street and Yale Avenue, this street fair that started in the 1890s has grown exponentially.

Today you will see nationally known musicians, extreme rides, and fun exhibits, for which Tulsa plays host to over one million visitors annually.

One of the main things people love about the Tulsa State Fair is the food! Try the moink balls, meatballs wrapped in bacon and dipped in BBQ sauce—your taste buds will thank you! Indulge in deep fried Twinkies or Oreos to satisfy your sweet tooth, and try the traditional funnel cakes and giant turkey legs. So in addition to seeing the animals, getting a ticket to ride something dangerous, and trying your luck at a game to win a giant stuffed animal, putting yourself into a food coma at the Tulsa State Fair is a favorite pastime of many.

Be sure to check out the Tulsa State Fair's Facebook page and website. Doing so will show you the specials for the day, including discounts on admission sponsored by local businesses.

www.tulsastatefair.com

3

HANG OUT
IN TRENDY BROOKSIDE

The supercool district of Brookside is located off Peoria Avenue between 31st and 51st Streets. Drive down into this very trendy neighborhood and you will find some of the best in food and drink at both local restaurants and national chains. Not only that, but Brookside also offers places to get a tattoo, pick out a special gift, or shop for a new outfit. Clothing, retail, and gift shops make Brookside a one-stop spot for all your needs.

Loaded with options for eating, you can have sushi, steak, tacos, Italian, or a variety of other special cuisines within a three-mile radius. In addition to popular stores like Trader Joe's you will find Tulsa exclusives like Ida Red General Store and Mondo's Italian Restaurant, a Tulsa tradition for over fifty years serving some of the best Italian cuisine the city.

For many amazing options, visit Brookside and enjoy what this area has to offer!

Author Recommendations in Brookside:

Brookside Tattoo—Jonathan
1143 E. 33rd Place, Tulsa, OK 74105
(918) 712-1122, www.brooksidetattoo.com

Ida Red
3336 S. Peoria Ave., Tulsa, OK 74105
(918) 949-6950, www.idaredgeneralstore.com

In the Raw Sushi
3321 S. Peoria Ave., Tulsa, OK 74105
(918) 744-1300, www.intherawsushi.com

Mondo's Ristorante Italiano
3410 S. Peoria Ave., Tulsa, OK 74105
(918) 561-6300

R Bar & Grill
3421 S. Peoria Ave., Tulsa, OK 74105
(918) 392-4811, www.rbartulsa.com

Slo Ride Brookside
4133 S. Peoria Ave., Tulsa, OK 74105
(918) 949-3393

4

RELISH
A RON'S HAMBURGER

Ron's has been a staple burger joint in Tulsa since 1975. Best known for their burgers and award-winning chili, Ron's has an extensive menu of comfort food that will leave you satisfied and definitely comforted.

What originally began as one man's dream to own a restaurant has now turned into a franchise with over twenty locations across Oklahoma, Arkansas, and Texas, many of which are family-owned and -operated, and it all started right here in Tulsa!

With five of those locations in the Tulsa area and suburbs alone, you can find one close to you and indulge in food that has been a tradition here for over three decades.

Ron's Hamburgers & Chili Locations:

1440 S. Denver Ave., Tulsa, OK 74119
(918) 382-7667

7119 S. Mingo Rd., Tulsa, OK 74133
(918) 250-7667

The Farm Shopping Center
6548 E. 51st St., Tulsa, OK 74135
(918) 664-5688

1545 S. Sheridan Rd., Tulsa, OK 74136
(918) 0832-1911

8201 S. Harvard Ave., Tulsa OK 74137
(918) 496-4328

Other locations in Jenks, Broken Arrow, Owasso,
Skiatook, Glenpool, and Claremore, OK

5

PARTAKE
IN A FOOD TRUCK SERIES

Lately, it seems that the number of food trucks available in Tulsa has really jumped, and the variety of food that you can get from them is amazing.

In downtown Tulsa you will find food trucks along the busy sidewalks on any weekend night and sometimes during weekdays as well. Everything—from street tacos to artisan pizzas—is available without having to wait for a table. Food trucks gather for a myriad of events where the vendors offer many wonderful choices to tantalize your taste buds.

Events like the East Street Tulsa Food Truck Festival showcase these movable feasts at various locations around the city for your tasting pleasure.

A few places, like Guthrie Green and Fuel 66 in Tulsa, host a regular food truck series. Check local papers, social media, and websites for exact dates and times.

Fuel 66 Tulsa
2439 E. 11th St., Tulsa, OK 74104
(918) 861-4110

Guthrie Green
111 E. Reconciliation Way, Tulsa, OK 74103
(918) 574-2421

6

TAKE IN THE SIGHTS AND SOUNDS
OF THE BLUE DOME DISTRICT

Getting its name from the historic 1924 Blue Dome Building, this district is known as an entertainment hub in the downtown area. Located at 2nd Street and Elgin Avenue, the blocks that make up this neighborhood combine great food, arcades, bowling, bars, and shopping into a compact and fun experience.

This unique district, home to festivals, runs, and competitions, offers a lively nightlife scene with a laid-back vibe. The annual St. Patrick's Day and Mardi Gras parades and festivals are held in this vibrant sector as well.

One of the most scenic rooftop dining experiences can be had in the Blue Dome district. Just a few blocks from the Blue Dome itself stands the historic building that is now home to El Guapo's Mexican restaurant. There is something for everyone on the menu, and the rooftop views are some of the best in downtown Tulsa.

www.bluedomedistrict.com

7

INDULGE IN INCREDIBLE OPTIONS ON CHERRY STREET

The Cherry Street District is a mile-long section off East 15th Street between Peoria and Lewis Avenues. It is chock-full of one-of-a-kind businesses, eating establishments, retail shops, and historic buildings. Its name comes directly from the original plats of the city.

Cherry Street was Tulsa's red-light district in the '30s and '40s, but is now a modern hub for exceptional dining experiences, bookstores, and vintage clothing shops. The district boasts some of the most unique shopping and restaurant finds in all of Tulsa.

Historic buildings line the street, and classic restaurants like Kilkenny's Irish Pub can be found there. With the undoubtedly largest menu in all of Tulsa and the welcoming atmosphere, this classic eatery will make you swoon! Grab some friends and prepare to be blown away by all the choices and options at this establishment alone!

I highly recommend taking a stroll with friends or family along this historic mile of shops and eateries in Tulsa. With so many options for food and drinks along Cherry Street, you can rest assured that you will find something to your liking.

8

EXPLORE THE 'BURBS
ON A DAY TRIP

Although Tulsa is an easy city to navigate, a short drive in any direction will take you to interesting neighboring cities and small towns that offer their own unique attractions to make a day trip worth your while.

Within a short fifteen- to twenty-minute drive, you can check out the old downtown of Sand Springs, Sapulpa, Broken Arrow, Owasso, or Catoosa. Visiting these smaller towns, you will notice less traffic and congestion, and you can shop, dine, play, and discover new things without the distractions common to bigger cities.

So hop in the car and drive thirty minutes (or, if you have the time, a couple of hours to our capital Oklahoma City) to explore what else the great state of Oklahoma has to offer. Whichever direction you decide to take, you are sure to find many new things to do that you will want to check off on your bucket list.

In these quaint suburbs you will find delicious food and drinks. In Broken Arrow's Rose District, there are a few small amazing specialty restaurants like the Rooftop, Toast, and Main Street Tavern, all of which are locally owned and operated. Catoosa has bragging rights to the best burgers at Flo's Burger Diner, and Hapa Japanese Cuisine and Baja Jacks are worth the short drive to Owasso.

RISE EARLY
FOR THE TULSA FARMERS MARKET

Not many things are worth getting up early for on a Saturday morning, but the Tulsa Farmers Market is definitely one of them! This twenty-year tradition in Tulsa is where you will find the freshest fruits, vegetables, and salsa mixes direct from local farmers. You can also get great local wines and cheeses, fresh flowers, plants, and handcrafted goods.

The Tulsa Farmers Market is a way for consumers to work directly with local farmers and, in turn, promote the community and economy. Several markets are offered throughout the city.

The Tulsa Farmers Market boasts over seventy-five local vendors whose products are 100% locally sourced, meaning that everything you buy is made here in Oklahoma or came directly from the soil of our wonderful state!

Be aware, however, that the markets are seasonal and only open on certain days at certain times. Although subject to change, a listing of dates and times are listed below.

Brookside Farmers Market
Wednesdays from May through September
7:30 a.m.–11:00 a.m.
Brookside Church—36th St. & Peoria Ave.

Cherry Street Farmers Market
Saturdays, April through October
7:00 a.m.–11:00 a.m.
15th St. & Peoria Ave. Parking Lot

info@tulsafarmersmarket.org
(918) 636-8419
P.O. Box 14572, Tulsa, OK 74159

10

SIP ON A NOSTALGIC MUG OF COFFEE

AT THE HIP GYPSY COFFEE HOUSE

The next time you want a cup of java, don't head to a national chain. Instead, consider sipping your joe in a nostalgic 1906 building that is now the Gypsy Coffee House. For the past eighteen years, this quiet coffee house has offered some of the best local coffee, espresso, and tea and demonstrations by local artists to be had in the city of Tulsa.

Decorated to project a bohemian vibe, this coffee house and cybercafé is a must-try for patrons looking for a quiet atmosphere, and the amazing aroma makes it a pleasant place to comfortably spend an hour or two lost in a book or visiting with a friend.

Muffins, pastries, and other delectable treats are also available at the Gypsy.

Open mic nights and poetry readings can be attended there and, when the weather is fine, the Gypsy has a nice outdoor patio, too.

Whatever brings you into the Gypsy, prepare to be mesmerized by her ambiance. This welcoming coffee house pulls you in, sits you down, and makes you want to linger.

303 Martin Luther King Jr. Blvd., Tulsa, OK 74103
(918) 295-2181, www.gypsycoffee.com

SHOP 'TIL YOU DROP
AT THE MOTHER ROAD MARKET

On the southwest corner of 11th Street and Lewis Avenue sits a new building named "Mother Road Market." It is Tulsa's very first food hall, with over twenty food and retail vendors under one roof. There is an impressive variety of food available and several vendors sell local merchandise, or related items, making Mother Road a great place to sip, shop, and eat all in one spot.

Built in 2018, the market has a nonprofit operation that helps food entrepreneurs grow and scale their businesses. Located in the building is Kitchen 66, Tulsa's kick-start kitchen and very first food incubator. These innovators help local entrepreneurs by providing them affordable kitchen space and all their essential needs, including the training programs and resources to help people grow their food business.

1124 S. Lewis Ave., Tulsa, OK 74104
(918) 984-9001

Hours:
Closed Monday
Tuesday–Thursday and Sunday 10:00 a.m.–9:00 p.m.
Friday and Saturday 10:00 a.m.–10:00 p.m.

12

TREAT YOURSELF TO A ROOFTOP VISTA IN DOWNTOWN TULSA

There are only a few places in Tulsa where you can enjoy a rooftop view. The skyline of Tulsa is unlike any other and is very recognizable for its art deco buildings and the eye-catching turquoise top of the Mid-Continent Tower.

One of the few places to see the skyline is El Guapo's Mexican Restaurant at 1st Street and Elgin Avenue. There is limited seating on the rooftop, so it's best to get there early to catch the best views of downtown Tulsa while enjoying some delicious Mexican cuisine.

Another hidden gem is the Roof Sixty-Six rooftop bar at the Indigo Hotel. Directly across the street from El Guapo's, their roof is a quite a bit taller, with a vast open view of downtown Tulsa.

The Mayo Hotel, where Elvis once stayed, has a penthouse bar, now open to the public. Here you not only get amazing views of the Tulsa skyline but also get signature cocktails in a 5-star historic hotel.

Whichever rooftop you choose, enjoy the city landscape and let the architecture and sights of one of America's most beautiful cities beguile you.

El Guapo's
332 E. 1st St., Tulsa, OK 74120
(918) 382-7482

Roof Sixty-Six Rooftop Bar
121 S. Elgin Ave., Tulsa, OK 74120
(918) 779-4445

Mayo Hotel—Penthouse Bar
115 W. 5th St., Tulsa, OK 74103
(918) 582-6296

13

SAVOR
MOUTHWATERING, AUTHENTIC, MEXICAN STREET TACOS

Though many places try, few can boast an outstanding carne asada taco. Luckily, the lovely city of Tulsa is privileged to be home to some authentic but not-so-well-known taco places as well as some upscale chain restaurants which serve the most delicious street tacos you can find anywhere. And if your Spanish is a little rusty, some of the restaurants offer picture menus to help you communicate your order.

So to enjoy some of the most amazing street tacos in the country, here is the ultimate go-to list for Tulsa. Even the chain restaurants get into the competitive spirit, and their street tacos rival those made in family-owned taquerias. The first one listed below is especially good—it has been a personal favorite of mine for several years.

Tacos El Rinconcito
4705 S. Braden Ave., Tulsa, OK 74135
(918) 576-6087

Taqueria la Cabana
10301 E. 51st St., Tulsa, OK 74146
(918) 610-8244

Louie's Grill & Bar
Several locations in Tulsa and Broken Arrow
6310 S. 101st St., Tulsa, OK 74137
(918) 298-5777

Chimi's Mexican Restaurant
Three locations in Tulsa
1304 E. 15th St., Tulsa, OK 74120
(918) 587-4411
www.chimismexican.com

14

SAMPLE THE CRAFT BREWS
ON A PUB CRAWL

Several different agencies run pub crawls in the Tulsa area. A pub crawl is usually a group of people with a common interest who get together and visit a few local watering holes on a timed assignment. There are trivia pub crawls, haunted bar crawls, alumni bar crawls, the Crawl for Cancer, the Blue Dome Sunday Funday Pub Crawl, and many others.

Partaking in a pub crawl is a really fun way to see the city and meet new people. Many of the pub crawls have different themes like Christmas Vacation, Toga Party, Back to the '80s, and other creative ideas for a different kind of night out.

Checking out the local taverns is a great way to meet like-minded people while sampling the local beers and craft cocktails made by talented Tulsa bartenders. If it's a pub crawl for charity, that makes it even better to participate.

Another interesting thing about attending a pub crawl is that the sponsors generally have deals for drinks or food worked out with the venues on the crawl. For one price, you can usually get tasty food, nicely paired beverages, friendly camaraderie, and a super fun time.

Crawl for Cancer
Offered annually, usually in April.
Check website for dates and times.
www.crawlforcancer.org

Haunted Pub Crawl by Tulsa Spirit Tours
Check website for dates and availability.
www.tulsaspirittour.com

The Office & Friends Trivia Pub Crawls
Dates vary.
www.crawlwith.us

DO THE CHICKEN DANCE
AT THE LINDE OKTOBERFEST

Every October for over forty years, people have come from far and wide to attend the Linde Oktoberfest in Tulsa. Thousands gather at the River West Festival Park to have their fill of beer, brats, food, arts, and entertainment.

Every year you can find German bands, games, competitions, authentic Bavarian cuisine, crafts, and lots of beer on the festival grounds in late October. The festival is based on the Munich Oktoberfest in Bavaria, Germany and was ranked one of the top five Oktoberfests in the nation by *USA Today* and one of the largest n America by Orbitz.

When you go, you will see how the community embraces this event, with people dressing in Bavarian costumes just to attend. Fill yourself up on bratwurst and beer and enjoy the sights, sounds, and German culture that are Oktoberfest.

Linde Oktoberfest
www.tulsaoktoberfest.org
Check website for exact dates

PROMENADE ON THE RIVERWALK
IN JENKS, USA

On the west side of the Arkansas River just across the East 96th Street bridge is Jenks, America. This sleepy little suburb offers quaint antique shops, the Oklahoma Aquarium, and another amazing resource named the Jenks Riverwalk.

The Riverwalk was the first development by the Muscogee Creek Nation to promote river revitalization. It connects Riverpark trails with dining, playing, and shopping activities to further enjoy life by the river.

On nice evenings the waterfront is lit up and teeming with people enjoying free outdoor concerts, shopping, and more, making it a destination all its own. The riverwalk is open year-round with indoor and outdoor activities and seating for some of Tulsa's best locally owned restaurants like Andolini's Pizza and Burn Co. Barbeque. In addition, Los Cabos Mexican Grill and Cantina has a large outdoor stage where you can enjoy local live entertainment while enjoying delicious Mexican cuisine. Waterfront Grill is nearby for a steak that will make your mouth water, and the Bramble is a bar serving breakfast that will start your day off right. Whichever you choose, you will not be disappointed.

300 Riverwalk Terrace, Jenks, OK 74037
(918) 409-8089, www.riverwalktulsa.com

17

TOUR
TULSA'S CRAFT BREWERIES

With craft beer becoming increasingly popular, microbreweries are popping up everywhere. Many people are finding that their weekend hobby of making craft beer can turn into a career opportunity and have invested in a brick and mortar brewery. These days, there are several different breweries around Tulsa offering an immense variety in specialty beers.

Craft beer can be an acquired taste, so many of the places offer other beverages to enjoy such as wine, soda, or cider. However, if you don't try one of their hand-crafted beers, you might be missing out on the main point of going to a microbrewery. You do not have to be a beer aficionado to enjoy the variety you can find around town.

In Tulsa you can take a brewery tour or just spend an afternoon visiting a few to see for yourself what the fuss is about. Finding a good craft beer to enjoy while supporting the community and its entrepreneurs is always a good thing.

Author Favorites:

Prairie BrewPub
223 N. Main St., Tulsa, OK
(918) 936-4395, www.prairiepub.com

Welltown Brewery
114 W. Archer St., Tulsa, OK
(918) 221-8893, www.welltownbrewing.com/weltown-brewing

Bricktown Brewery
9409 E. 71st St., Tulsa, OK 74133
(918) 994-4456, www.bricktownbrewery.com

Pearl Brewery Tours
424 S. Utica Ave., Tulsa, OK 74104
(918) 403-9483, www.pearlbrewerytours.com

Cabin Boys Brewery
1717 E. 7th St., Tulsa, OK 74104
(918) 933-4033, www.cabinboysbrewery.com

Broken Arrow Brewery
333 W. Dallas St., Broken Arrow, OK 74012
(918) 286-8101, www.brokenarrowbrewingco.com

18

DISCOVER THE BEST PIZZA IN TULSA

Tulsa has several hidden treasures when it comes to pizzerias in the city. Since everyone has different taste and each person has their own favorite style of pie, each of the places mentioned here has its own take on how to master a pizza and luckily for Tulsans, these pizza crafters are all within easy reach. For this author, a good pie consists of tasty sauce, ample cheese and toppings, and a decent size slice. A good deal is also at the top of the priority list for most folks on a budget.

Some of the pizzerias mentioned are family-owned and specific to Tulsa, so not many people know about them. They help make Tulsa unique, and visiting these locations helps contribute to the thriving economy of our city.

Here are my top five pizza places, chosen because they have the best Italian-inspired recipes for pizza in Tulsa.

Andolini's Pizzeria
1552 E. 15th St., Tulsa, OK 74120
(918) 728-6111
Other locations in Broken Arrow, Owasso and Jenks

Pie Hole Pizzeria
2708 E. 15th St., Tulsa, OK 74104
(918) 742-1200

NY Style Pizza
4775 S. Harvard Ave., Tulsa OK 74135
(918) 779-7760

Bohemian Pizza
818 E. 3rd St., Tulsa, OK 74120
(918) 895-6999, www.eastvillagebohemian.com

Umberto's
3147 S. Harvard Ave., Tulsa, OK 74134
(918) 712-1999

19

DEVELOP YOUR PALATE

AT THE LOCAL WINERIES AND WINE BARS

For those who prefer wine to beer, the city of Tulsa offers a few select wineries and wine bars that host tastings and wine pairings for the sophisticated palate. If you are looking to be educated in the wine-making process, a trip to a local vineyard allows you to learn about the region that the specific grapes come from, what wines pair well with different foods, and how to make and ferment small batches of your favorite styles of vino. Some wineries even provide outdoor seating in the vineyards themselves for an aesthetically pleasing meal on a special occasion.

Some local wineries have gift shops and tasting rooms where good wine can be sampled and purchased to take home. Others offer food so you can make an entire afternoon out of learning about wine, sipping your favorites, and enjoying a well-prepared meal in an atmosphere that is warm, inviting, and educational.

Waters Edge Winery & Bistro
116 S. Main St., Broken Arrow, OK 74012
www.wewba.com

Whispering Vines Vineyard
7374 W. 51st St., Tulsa, OK 74107
(918) 447-0808

The Wine Loft Bar
7890 E. 106th Pl. S., Suite 14, Tulsa, OK 74133
(918) 970-4766

Doc's Wine & Food
3509 S. Peoria Ave., Tulsa, OK 74105
(918) 949-3663, www.docswineandfood.com

MEET FRIENDS FOR BREAKFAST
AT TALLY'S CAFÉ

A '50s style diner on Route 66 that has been a staple in Tulsa since 1987 is Tally's Café. Tally's serves breakfast, lunch, and dinner in a neon-filled, open-concept diner with a variety of fresh American fare. With over one hundred comfort-food dishes to choose from, you are sure to find something to satisfy your taste buds.

Tally Alame, founder and owner of the café, has an amazing story of escaping the civil war in Lebanon to find the true American dream. He has won awards for Tulsa's Best Breakfast, Tulsa's Best Diner, and Tulsa's Best Cinnamon Rolls, and there is a reason for that: Tally's is simply the best!

However, he is also known locally for a notable act of kindness: Tally once served a free Thanksgiving dinner to the homeless just weeks after opening his doors. He gave back to the community and has continued that tradition throughout the years.

So grab some friends and head to Tally's for a Tulsa tradition that should be shared. However, plan to get there early to avoid the massive crowds that also know about where to get great breakfast in Tulsa.

TIP

Try the enormous and delicious cinnamon buns, but be warned—they are huge and you will want to share! Tally's also has some fun brunch cocktails and shots on the menu. Enjoy a mimosa, Tally's spicy Bloody Mary, or an Irish coffee. If you're really brave, try one of their breakfast shots like Jameson and butterscotch schnapps served with OJ and bacon.

Open daily from 6:00 a.m.–11:00 p.m.

Tally's Café

1102 S. Yale Ave., Tulsa, OK 74112

(918) 835-8039

6100 S. Sheridan Rd., Tulsa, OK 74133

(918) 895-6375

GET INTO YOUR LEAGUE
AT THE DUST BOWL

The Dust Bowl Lanes & Lounge is located in the Pearl District at the corner of 2nd Street and Elgin Avenue. This local hot spot is a place where you can enjoy bowling, good food, and drinks and still feel like you had a big-city night out. The uniqueness of this retro-inspired venue is its 1970s décor that mimics the bowling alleys of days gone by. The Dust Bowl offers late hours, a full bar, and thumping music for a fun night out. This is not your father's bowling alley!

As you soak in the vintage vibe, enjoy delicious burgers, hot dogs, sandwiches, salads, and shakes in this nostalgic locale. After 8:00 p.m. you must be twenty-one or over to enter.

As stated on their website, "Dust Bowl Lanes & Lounge is a retro-inspired tribute to the bowling alleys and lounges of the 1970s located in Tulsa, OKC, and Little Rock (Arkansas)." At Dust Bowl, a little nostalgia goes a long way.

211 S. Elgin Ave., Tulsa, OK 74120
(918) 430-3901, www.dustbowllounge.com

Hours:
Saturday 12:00 p.m.–2:00 a.m.
Sunday 12:00 p.m.–12:00 a.m.
Monday through Thursday 4:00 p.m.–2:00 a.m.

FISH AROUND FOR THE BEST SEAFOOD

Oklahoma is about as far away from the ocean as you can get, so when it comes to fresh seafood, it's imperative to find a place where freshness overrides everything. Only two places in Tulsa have bragging rights about the caliber of the seafood they serve.

The first is the White River Fish Market and Seafood Restaurant. This local legend has served Tulsa since 1932. In an inconspicuous strip mall near the Tulsa International Airport, you will find a cafeteria-style restaurant that you would never suspect serves Tulsa's freshest seafood. Looks can be deceiving where this place is concerned, but the line of customers out the door is a testament to White River's commitment to fresh food.

The second place in Tulsa that has bragging rights to the best seafood is Bodean's. This seafood treasure started in 1968 as a market and wholesale distributor. Over the past few decades they have developed a fabulous fine-dining restaurant experience with an award-winning food and wine menu.

White River Fish Market & Restaurant
1708 N. Sheridan Rd., Tulsa, OK 74115
(918) 835-1910

Bodean's Seafood Restaurant & Market
3376 E. 51st St., Tulsa, OK 74135
(918) 749-1407

23

TEASE YOUR TASTE BUDS
AT ONE OF TULSA'S GOURMET BURGER JOINTS

Tulsa is a test market hub for new restaurants, so we've seen a few fly-by-night burger joints. Only the best survive the test of time, and we are fortunate to have some of those restaurants in our midst.

Brownie's Hamburger Stand, an icon in Tulsa, has been serving up delicious food since 1956. Brownie's is one of the oldest burger joints in town. It is open seven days a week and provides good food, good service, and some of the best burgers you can find in T-town.

Ty's Burgers on South Harvard Avenue and Arnold's Old-Fashioned Burgers at 51st Street and Union Avenue are some of Tulsa's best kept secrets for a good burger. Both of them still make everything fresh the old-fashioned way, which explains how they have maintained their quality for so many years. The Mom and Pop feel and dated décor give you a nostalgic feeling while you satisfy your burger craving.

Brownie's Hamburger Stand
Several locations around Tulsa
2130 S. Harvard Ave., Tulsa, OK 74114
(918) 744-0320

Ty's Hamburgers
1534 S. Harvard Ave., Tulsa, OK 74112
(918) 749-8122

Fat Guy's Burger Bar
140 N. Greenwood Ave., Tulsa, OK 74120
(918) 794-7782

Arnold's Old-Fashioned Burgers
4253 Southwest Blvd., Tulsa, OK 74107
(918) 445-4633

THE HUNT CLUB
224
Miller
HIGH LIFE
$3 DRAFTS ALL DAY EVERYDAY!

MUSIC AND ENTERTAINMENT

24

TICKLE YOUR FANCY
AT THE AWARD-WINNING BOK CENTER

The Bank of Oklahoma Center, or BOK Center as it's known, is a 19,199-seat arena. This large venue hosts a variety of events from indoor hockey, basketball, and arena football games to sold-out music concerts. Many famous acts have performed on the stage: KISS, Def Leppard, Madonna, Stevie Nicks, Elton John, Billy Joel, George Strait, and Fleetwood Mac, just to name a few. Many of these acts even started their world tours right here in Tulsa at the amazing BOK Center.

The venue has won several "Arena of the Year" awards, beating out other famous venues including Madison Square Garden in New York City. It's also had the honor of being ranked seventh in a poll of the top hundred concert venues in the country. Not bad for little ole Tulsa!

So when you get the chance, go see a good show hosted by the BOK. Enjoy the food and beverages at over fourteen concession outlets throughout the 565,000-square-foot facility and enjoy a show like you've never seen before.

200 S. Denver Ave., Tulsa, OK 74103
(918) 894-4200, www.bokcenter.com

Box Office Hours:
Monday–Friday, 10:00 a.m.–5:00 p.m.
Evening, weekend, and holiday hours vary according to event schedule.

BRAVE THE DARK SIDE OF TULSA

WITH TULSA SPIRIT TOURS

Every city has a fascinating and dark past, and most of them offer tours that tell you about their macabre histories. In Tulsa, we've come a long way from unjustly hanging people in the street, but some claim the ghosts of those unfortunate people still remain.

Tulsa Spirit Tours began in 2003 when a woman with a vision and great story-telling ability decided to host the first ever "Haunted History Tour" in Tulsa. Renting a trolley and gathering spooky stories, small bits of personal experience, and local folklore and history, she set out teach the citizens of Tulsa about the past of their city that isn't so well known.

Celebrating sixteen years of haunted history tours, Tulsa Spirit Tours offers adventures that will educate, excite, and astound you with local legends and eerie facts from long ago, highlighting "the good, the bad, and the ugly" past of T-town.

www.tulsaspirittours.com, www.facebook.com/tulsaspirittours
(918) 694-7488

TIP

Walking tours run year-round, and bus tours run seasonally. Check website for current schedule. Private tours offered for groups.

26

CATCH A FLICK ON THE LAWN
AT GUTHRIE GREEN

Located in the heart of Tulsa's vibrant arts district is a large inviting green space taking up an entire city block that includes a lawn, restaurant, dock, and performance stage. The Guthrie Green is a diverse urban social space where everyone is welcome. It opened in September of 2012 and hosts concerts, festivals, and performing arts, all of them free to the public.

Every Thursday from May through October, the green hosts a Movie in the Park night and sets up a large screen so patrons can watch a flick under the stars. The movies usually start around 8:30 p.m. and often have ties to Oklahoma or Tulsa specifically. Regardless of the movie being shown, you can almost be guaranteed a good time, a good vibe, and a relaxing evening on the lawn. Food trucks are often available, but you are also welcome to bring your own snacks to enjoy with your flick.

Bring a blanket and enjoy the show.

111 Reconciliation Way, Tulsa, OK 74103
(918) 574-2421

TOUR
THE TULSA CAVE HOUSE

Just west of downtown Tulsa on Charles Page Boulevard is an unusual rock structure known as the Tulsa Cave House. Built in the 1920s as the "Cave Garden" restaurant, it was rumored to have had some of the best fried chicken you could find this side of the Mississippi River. However, this little chicken restaurant had a lot more to offer its patrons if you knew the right password. Turns out there was a speakeasy behind the chicken restaurant façade. During Prohibition, it was a magical place of dining, dancing, and drinking neatly tucked underground and away from prying eyes and ears.

Since then, it's been a private residence and a resale shop. There were fifteen owners before Linda Collier purchased the unusual structure in 1997. Since that time, she has lovingly restored the old house and learned its fascinating history, which she tells while giving tours.

Check the Tulsa Cave House Facebook page for posted tour times (as they vary) or call for a private tour.

1623 Charles Page Blvd., Tulsa, OK 74127
(918) 378-1952, www.facebook.com/thecaveintulsa

SING ALONG
AT A FREE SUMMERTIME OUTDOOR CONCERT

Tulsa has been favorably compared to cities like Memphis and Nashville when it comes to the local music scene. The amazing musical talent available in Tulsa is as diverse as its people, and if you haven't had the chance to hear these skilled musicians, the Summer Concert Series is a great way to do that.

There are several places in Tulsa that host free outdoor concerts in the summertime. The sheer number of concerts offered around the city guarantees that you will be able to find many with diverse styles of music that fit into your busy summer schedule.

The summer concerts are a great time. Bring a blanket, lawn chair, and a friend to experience the camaraderie that music affords to people from all walks of life and enjoy an evening of good music and community spirit in a relaxed, casual atmosphere.

Most concerts are from 7:00 to 9:00 p.m. but check local websites for accurate times, dates, and updates.

Tulsa Summertime Concert Series

Summer's Fifth Night at Utica Square
2070 Utica Square, Tulsa, OK 74114
(918) 742-5531, www.uticasquare.com/events

Starlight Band Summer Concerts & Sunday Concerts in the Park
Guthrie Green
111 Reconciliation Way, Tulsa, OK 74103
(918) 574-2421
www.guthriegreen.com/events-calendar

LaFortune Park Concert Series
Gardens at LaFortune
5202 S. Hudson Ave., Tulsa, OK 74135
(918) 496-6220
www.parks.tulsacounty.org/parks.aspx?page=lafortune

Rose District, Broken Arrow
Main Street Pavilion, Downtown
418 S. Main St., Broken Arrow, OK 74012
(918) 451-2815

Jenks Riverwalk Concert Series
Riverwalk Crossing
300 Riverwalk Terrace, Jenks, OK 74037
(918) 409-8089

29

DEBATE THE LOCATION
OF THE CENTER OF THE UNIVERSE

Okay, okay, while I don't know if it's *actually* the center of the universe, some claim that it is.

At the top of the bridge at Archer Street and Boston Avenue, you will find a circle of thirteen rows of bricks that causes a mysterious acoustic phenomenon. If you stand in the center and talk, there is an unusual reverberation effect to your voice that only you can hear. The curvature of the bricks and outlying concrete benches are said to be the cause.

Originally built in the 1930s for vehicles, the bridge was destroyed by fire in the 1980s but rebuilt as a pedestrian bridge. During the reconstruction, a circular design of bricks was placed on the expansion joint, causing the happy and unexpected anomaly. This fun phenomenon attracts thousands of visitors, and rumors have surfaced about it being set at the exact longitude and latitude of the center of the universe—but I will let you do the math!

There have also been many crazy theories to try and explain this weird acoustic oddity. Whatever the case, the abnormality seems to defy the laws of physics.

Boston Avenue Pedestrian Bridge, Downtown Tulsa

AWAKEN YOUR SENSES
AT A FIRST FRIDAY ART CRAWL

The Tulsa Arts District hosts a monthly event, year-round, that showcases local artists and gives them an opportunity to display and sell their art. Local food trucks line the street and curbside musicians contribute to a fun night of music, food, and art. What started in 2007 as the First Friday Art Crawl has now become a staple event in the downtown area.

As the name suggests, on the first Friday of every month the local galleries and studios open their doors, and mini-galleries pop up along the streets where thousands stroll through a myriad of art offerings such as paintings, jewelry, pottery, and more. Each piece showcases the emotional application of an individual artist's vision or personal story.

The First Friday Art Crawl was voted the best public entertainment event in the city. Plan an evening with friends to share an exciting experience in visual and performing arts while showing support for local Tulsa artists.

First Friday Art Crawl
First Friday of every month in the Tulsa Arts District,
Reconciliation Way & Main St.
6:00 p.m.–9:00 p.m.

31

SPEND AN EVENING WITH FRIENDS IN THE TULSA ARTS DISTRICT

The Tulsa Arts District has much to offer on any given night. What were once abandoned warehouses are now revitalized buildings full of life in the form of restaurants, night clubs, art galleries, and event spaces. Two local breweries call the district home and a variety of restaurants, bars, and clubs guarantee that you will never be lacking for something to do. Go dancing, enjoy a local live band, eat, shop, and play in a historic district that showcases local artists and entrepreneurs.

Take a haunted history tour of the oldest business district in Tulsa, or watch the Tulsa Drillers ballgame and fireworks show. Attend a concert at the award-winning BOK Center after having dinner at a secret speakeasy hidden in a nearby alley.

All of downtown is vibrant and eclectic, but you will find yourself especially drawn to the nostalgic beauty of the Tulsa Arts District and it will call you back for more.

CHECK OUT THE ECLECTIC VIBE OF DOWNTOWN TULSA

Many people who have been in Tulsa most of their lives remember when downtown was only open for business during the day, leaving empty sidewalks and abandoned buildings at night. However, downtown has experienced a resurgence and there's a whole different ambiance now.

Where once the streets were desolate and lonely, you can now find areas that treat you to fireworks, art, music, or festivals and some of the best food and drinks in the state. You can try your hand at gambling or explore a secret speakeasy. Watch glass being blown while eating decadent handmade chocolates or treat yourself to some amazing locally sourced fare.

Downtown Tulsa is made up of several different districts. Each one offers a diverse culture unique to the district in terms of art, music, food, entertainment, retail, and history. In addition, tours are offered in many districts that entertain participants with the rich and colorful history of Tulsa.

Throughout downtown you will find historic theaters and buildings that coexist comfortably beside new museums, restaurants, retail businesses, and housing spaces. Downtown is diverse and eclectic, and the revitalization buzz is seriously invigorating.

BE A WITNESS TO SOCIAL JUSTICE
AT THE WOODY GUTHRIE CENTER

Oklahoma native Woody Guthrie is an American singer and songwriter most known for his famous song "This Land Is Your Land." He has been an inspiration to many people because he practiced what he preached about diversity, social justice, and equality in his powerful folk music.

The Woody Guthrie Center is a museum dedicated to spreading Woody's words of hope and truth. It honors his life and legacy in a pragmatic way, educating visitors about his message. You can attend concerts, workshops, and other events hosted at the venue and learn about the message it shares in hopes of affecting positive change.

Visit the Woody Guthrie Center for an evening of creative displays and special gallery exhibits that show you what a true cultural icon Woody Guthrie was to America.

102 Reconciliation Way, Tulsa OK 74103
(918) 574-2710, www.woodyguthriecenter.org
info@woodyguthriecenter.org

Tuesday–Sunday 10:00 a.m.–6:00 p.m.
First Fridays of the month 10:00 a.m.–9:00 p.m.

EXPERIENCE
THE TULSA SOUND

Tulsa rivals Memphis and Nashville, Tennessee for producing and promoting quality music in its entertainment venues. Many famous musicians have come out of Tulsa, and a lot of good, diverse, and polished music is generated here.

The Tulsa Sound, as it's been called, came about in the 1950s and infuses country, rock, blues, and rock-a-billy music into its own entity. This popular style of music was made famous by the likes of J. J. Cale, Eric Clapton, Leon Russell, and Elvin Bishop. Today that style is unique and hard to find, but a few talented local artists are keeping it alive by giving us their own version of the true "Tulsa Sound."

Check around for local bars and taverns that promote Tulsa-style bands and get ready to get down and feel the beat.

The Paul Benjamin Band
www.paulbenjamanband.com/music
www.facebook.com/pbenjamanband

The Brothers Moore
www.facebook.com/thebrothersmoore

Mercury Lounge
1747 South Boston Ave.
(918) 770-9826, www.mercurylounge918.com

35

TRY YOUR LUCK
AT A LOCAL CASINO

Tulsa is home to a few American Indian casinos: River Spirit, Osage, and Hard Rock.

Perhaps good fortune will be on your side. With a positive mental attitude and a few extra dollars, you never know! However, the casinos aren't just for gambling. Their food, entertainment, and night life are top-notch. From magic shows to concerts to comedians, these casinos host them all.

If you are not ready to challenge the house by gambling, people-watching is another fun part of the casino experience. Quietly sliding up next to an intense poker game or seeing someone hit a large jackpot and watching the machine go crazy is exhilarating, even if you aren't the lucky recipient of the winnings.

With so much to do, it's fun to schedule a date night or night out with friends or family to enjoy the many bars and restaurants throughout the casino buildings. Go have some fun and enjoy the excitement that the local casinos have to offer. And should you decide to gamble, may Lady Luck be on your side.

River Spirit Casino Resort
8330 Riverside Pkwy., Tulsa, OK 74137
(918) 299-8518

Hard Rock Hotel & Casino Tulsa
777 W. Cherokee St., Catoosa, OK 74015
(800) 760-6700

Osage Hotel and Casino
951 W. 36th St. N., Tulsa, OK 74127
(877) 246-8777

Osage Casino
301 Blackjack, Sand Springs, OK 74063
(877) 246-8777

36

CHILL OUT
IN AN UNDERGROUND TUNNEL TOUR

The city of Tulsa has several mysterious tunnels that run underneath the city and connect certain buildings. The purpose behind those tunnels is both frightening and fascinating.

In the early 1900s, Tulsa was known as the Oil Capital of the World, making many people wealthy. Those with wealth and prestige needed a safe way to move about the city without fear of being kidnapped for ransom by gangsters like Machine-Gun Kelly. The tunnels were created so wealthy men could move between their offices and homesteads without being seen, as kidnapping and robbery were very real fears and distinct possibilities for those who were affluent. The tunnels today are painted, carpeted, and lighted, and tours can show you the hidden treasures still available there.

Tunnel tours are offered at different times depending on the season and the tour company. Be sure to check local websites or call for times, dates, and availability.

Tulsa Historical Society
2445 S. Peoria Ave., Tulsa, OK 74114
(918) 712-9484, www.tulsahistory.org/learn/programs-tours /educational-programs-for-adults/downtown-walking-tours

Tulsa Foundation for Architecture
633 S. Boston Ave., Tulsa, OK 74119
(918) 583-5550, www.tulsaarchitecture.org/programs/2nd -saturday-tulsa-underground-tunnel-tour

Tours of Tulsa
Kelly Gibson
(918) 625-4909, www.toursoftulsa.com

37

RAISE THE SPIRITS
AT HEX HOUSE

There is an empty lot at 10 East 21st Street directly across from Veterans Park that was the site of a bizarre string of events in the 1940s. The lot is supposedly cursed because of it.

Carolann Smith held two women captive in the basement of her home for eight years. The women claimed to be "mesmerized" by Smith and essentially programmed to do whatever she wanted them to do. During the execution of a search warrant for wartime ration fraud, the women were found and the news about this strange case spread quickly through the city.

The house where this enslavement took place was demolished in the 1970s, but the lot is still there and wild claims of it being haunted have surfaced. Cars are said to start without keys in the ignition, and other odd things have been reported.

So if you're brave enough, drive to the empty lot, turn off the car, remove the keys from the ignition, and see if anything happens—if you dare . . .

Original Hex House Location
10 E. 21st St., Tulsa, OK 74114

SAMPLE THE SHOPS AND EATERIES
IN BROKEN ARROW ROSE DISTRICT

Broken Arrow was the largest suburb of Tulsa according to the 2010 census. A legend says that early Native American settlers broke an arrow in two and offered it as a sign of peace, giving the town its name. Although the story turns out not to be true, it is an amusing and persistent urban legend nonetheless.

This growing suburb has experienced a surge in recent development in their downtown Rose District, and now it's a must-see. Small shops, boutiques, and eateries fill the historic buildings. There's also a pavilion with a splash pad in the summer and a skating rink in the winter.

Broken Arrow is also home to the famed Rooster Days Festival. This festival is a miniature state fair with all the delights of a large one: food, carnival rides, live entertainment, markets, and more. People come from all over to partake in the Rooster Days festivities held during Mother's Day weekend in May.

It's a short drive to Broken Arrow and a small price to pay to explore all this charming suburban fair has to offer.

Rose District
S. Main St., Broken Arrow, OK 74012

PARTY WITH THE STARS
AT THE OBSERVATORY

Located just south of the city, the Astronomy Club of Tulsa and its domed Observatory are perched on a small hilltop in Mounds, Oklahoma. Opened in 1993, the observatory offers monthly star parties, presentations, club meetings, and more. For a small donation, visitors can use the high-powered telescopes and learn about the stars in the ACT Observatory complex which houses a classroom, an entire acre for outdoor observation, and bathrooms.

Find constellations and learn about many different celestial objects and other space phenomena. Enjoy a quiet, dark night of stargazing with the Astronomy Club of Tulsa.

The observatory is only open to the public during certain times and can be closed due to inclement weather. Always check ahead on their website to be sure they are still open.

Astronomy Club of Tulsa Observatory
858 Ferguson Rd., Mounds, OK 74047
www.astrotulsa.com

Don’t use GPS navigation!
It often sends people on an inconvenient path of rugged, impassable, or nonexistent roads. For a map and specific directions please visit the website at www.astrotulsa.com.

The observatory is only open for scheduled events and be sure to check the website for cancellations before heading out.

GO ON SAFARI
AT THE TULSA ZOO

The Tulsa Zoo has something for everyone. There you will find living museums in which indoor and outdoor open-air exhibits give visitors a clear view of the animals and also help them feel less caged in with more of a natural environment. The Tulsa Zoo's ongoing goal of wildlife conservation gives us an amazing display of animals including a tropical rain forest exhibit and a sea lion cove.

Plan to spend an entire day, because there is so much to see and do at the Tulsa Zoo. The zoo's directors and curators are always changing exhibits and creating different educational programs so it is a place that you can visit with your family again and again, seeing something new every time.

The zoo is open from 9:00 a.m. to 5:00 p.m., every day of the year except Christmas.

6421 E. 36th St. N., Tulsa, OK 44115
(918) 669-660

41

ENTER THE MIDGET CAR RACING WORLD

AT THE RENOWNED CHILI BOWL

A very popular event in Tulsa is the annual Chili Bowl race. Originally sponsored by the Chili Bowl food company, this midget car racing event draws hundreds of drivers from all forms of racing. People descend upon Tulsa from all over the world to be a part of this national event.

The Chili Bowl races started in 1987 and have been run every year since just two weeks after Christmas. NASCAR has acknowledged the race as a major event, and it has been dubbed the Super Bowl of Midget Car Racing. In addition, there is a large trade show, free to the public, which sells racing memorabilia, apparel, and more. You can also treat yourself to some delicious locally made pizza from Pizza Express, considered the official Chili Bowl pizza.

No need to bundle up, as this race is held indoors. Come comfortable and ready for a fun and exciting time.

Tulsa Fairgrounds
Tulsa Expo Raceway, 4145 E. 21st St., Tulsa, OK 74114
(918) 838-3777, www.chilibowl.com

42

LOAD UP ON COMFORT FOOD AND FUN
AT THE TULSA INTERNATIONAL MAYFEST

Mayfest is a four-day festival full of food, fun, and performing and visual arts. This massive festival that has been entertaining Tulsans since 1973 has thousands of visitors each year. For decades it was located in the Blue Dome District, but as of 2019 Mayfest was moved to the Tulsa Arts District.

Local and national artists and food vendors set up tents throughout the district where they offer a plethora of inviting objects and food options to appeal to all your senses. Professional and amateur artists with a serious love of their respective crafts provide diverse art, music, and visual galleries for you to treat yourself during this spring fling.

Mayfest generally occurs during the third week in May and sometimes coincides with other festivals going on downtown, adding to the list of fun activities to fill your spring weekends. The free event also includes a family-friendly KidsZone with activities for children of all ages.

111 E. Reconciliation Way, Tulsa, OK 74103
(918) 582-6435, www.tulsamayfest.org
www.facebook.com/tulsainternationalmayfest

ENJOY FILMS UNDER THE STARS
AT THE ADMIRAL TWIN DRIVE-IN

Back in 2010 this historic drive-in had a devastating fire that many believed would mark the end of Tulsa's outdoor movie theater era forever. However, thanks to crowd-sourcing, fundraisers, and the enthusiastic support of the Tulsa community, this iconic drive-in theater is back.

Originally built in 1951 and called the Modernaire, the name was changed when a second "twin" screen was added in 1955 and it became known as the Admiral Twin Drive-In.

Not only is the Admiral Twin Drive-In good for nostalgic reasons, but parts of the film *The Outsiders*, adapted from the book of the same name by Tulsa native S. E. Hinton, were filmed at this famous spot. You can sit on the same bench in front of the concession stand occupied by the character Ponyboy in one scene of the film.

Visit this iconic treasure for the classic concessions, experience a piece of cinematic history, and enjoy the grandeur of the really big screen from the comfort of your own vehicle.

The drive-in is open seasonally and all showtimes can be found on their website.

7355 E. Easton St.
(918) 878-8099, www.admiraltwindrivein.com

DEVELOP A TASTE FOR LIVE THEATER

AT THE TULSA PERFORMING ARTS CENTER

For some people, Tulsa may not conjure up visions of staged plays or musicals, but like most major cities throughout the country, our city has an artistic side with an extensive menu of drama, music, dance, and acting events. The PAC, as it's often called, is an elegant venue with offerings that have played on Broadway and beyond. Since 1977, it has hosted theatrical shows, concerts, lectures, dance, opera, and more.

Purchase a subscription to hear the season's symphony concerts or get individual tickets to take in a traditional musical or holiday classic with family. Whichever event you choose to attend, you will not be disappointed by the professionalism, the seating, or the acoustics.

Visit their website for a listing of current plays, shows and events.

110 E. 2nd St., Tulsa, OK 74103
(918) 596-7111, www.tulsapac.com

Ticket Office Hours:
Monday–Friday, 10:30 a.m.–5:30 p.m.

45

SPEND THE DAY
AT THE TULSA AIR AND SPACE MUSEUM & PLANETARIUM

Many people are aware that Tulsa was once known as the Oil Capital of the World, but very few people know that Tulsa had a huge role in the aviation industry as well, and we still do today.

The Tulsa Air and Space Museum & Planetarium opened in 1998 and now showcases aerospace history dating back to the early 1900s. From old aircraft to vintage uniforms and more, the Tulsa Air and Space Museum & Planetarium will surprise you with the many facts and artifacts on display in the impressive facility. The James E. Bertelsmeyer Planetarium was added in 2006 and hosts star shows and community events.

Here you can educate yourself about the local history of aeronautics and see a model of the original art deco Tulsa Municipal Terminal where legends like Will Rogers, Amelia Earhart, and Wiley Post passed through on their way into Tulsa. Hear about Oklahoma astronauts and pilots who've made history or see parts made right here in Tulsa that helped launch man into space.

Parking is free, but check the website in case of closings due to holidays or other events.

3624 N. 74th E. Ave., Tulsa, OK 74115
(918) 834-9900, info@tulsamuseum.org

Open Monday–Saturday 10:00 a.m.–4:00 p.m.

DISCOVER GILCREASE
AFTER HOURS

One of Tulsa's early philanthropists was Thomas Gilcrease. He acquired great wealth in the oil industry and with his money bought a massive collection of Native American art. That art is now displayed at the Gilcrease Museum in west Tulsa, a showcase for Native American pride. Adjacent to the museum sits an old two-story mansion that used to be the personal abode of Mr. Gilcrease. The house has a large wrap-around porch, lush landscaping, and a cascading fountain.

Today the house is mostly empty, but occasionally art classes are hosted there. However, on the last Friday of the month, local musicians play outdoors on the large Southern-style wrap-around porch in a free starlight concert. In addition, Gilcrease After Hours features food trucks and tents sponsored by local restaurants for this culture and cocktails event. Bring a friend and a lawn chair or a blanket, and enjoy an evening of music, food, and fun.

1400 N. Gilcrease Museum Rd., Tulsa, OK 74127
(918) 596-2700

Event is Free
7:00–9:00 p.m.
Last Friday of every month
(check website and Facebook page for verification)

47

FIND YOUR FAVORITE MUSICIANS

AT THE OKLAHOMA JAZZ HALL OF FAME

Many people don't realize we have a Jazz Hall of Fame right in our back yard. The Union Depot train station built in 1931 used to be the hub for the local railway system. It was used for that purpose until 1967, but after that the station was abandoned for nearly twenty years. Built during the Depression in the true art deco style that Tulsa is known for, this opulent building was a sign of hope in very uncertain times.

In 2007, due to a bond issue and private funding, the depot's resurgence began. Today it holds a museum that honors jazz performers and musicians and hosts jazz performances by artists from all over the world. Educational programs and initiatives are offered there as well.

Visit to learn about the famous inductees and listen to the easy-going jazz fusion that is considered America's classical music. You can get a feel for their motto of "Creating Unity Through Music" the second you walk through the doors of this beautifully restored landmark.

5 S. Boston Ave., Tulsa, OK 74103
(918) 928-JAZZ (5289), www.okjazz.org
www.jazzhalltickets.com

48

STEP BACK IN TIME
AT THE TULSA ART DECO MUSEUM

Tulsa is very well known for its Art Deco buildings, which can be found throughout the city. This popular design movement began in the 1920s and 1930s.

The Decopolis Tulsa Art Deco Museum is located in the lobby of the historic Philcade Building in downtown Tulsa. This museum displays an amazing collection from Tulsa's age, a testament to Tulsa's wealth, opulence, and rich art deco legacy. You can see artifacts, clothing, and other heirlooms on display from that unique era of design. The Philcade building itself is the epitome of art deco architecture and boasts some of the most breathtaking art deco installations you can find in the Tulsa area.

Admission is free and there is also a gift shop where you can purchase art deco replicas and other fun, informative, Tulsa-based books and mementos.

511 S. Boston Ave., Tulsa, OK 74103
(918) 382-7388

Lobby Exhibit Hours:
Monday–Friday: 8:00 a.m.–6:00 p.m.
Saturday: 11:00 a.m.–5:00 p.m.

Museum Store Hours:
Wednesday & Thursday: 11:00 a.m.–2:00 p.m.
Friday & Saturday: 11:00 a.m.–5:00 p.m.

FEEL THE NEED FOR SPEED
AT TULSA RACEWAY PARK

Originally opened in the 1960s as Tulsa International Raceway, this racing track has been in Tulsa for decades and is one of only fourteen tracks of that vintage still in use in the country. The races are an exciting way for people to get together in an open stadium and experience the heart-pumping, adrenalin-producing, one-of-a-kind excitement that only drag racing can give you.

Even if drag racing and race cars aren't your thing, it is an exhilarating experience and something you must try at least once! Check out the raceway's extensive list of events happening on any given night and you will surely find one to interest and entertain you.

3101 N. Garnett Rd., Tulsa, OK 74116
(918) 417-7223, www.tulsaracewaypark.com

50

TAKE
AN ARCHITECTURE AND ART DECO TOUR

In the downtown area you can take all kinds of tours to learn about the city's past, from architectural gems to the oil boom and more.

There are a few companies and non-profit organizations that offer regular tours of Tulsa's art deco buildings where you can learn about the city's rich history as a boomtown for some of the best architects in the country. Many places around the downtown area also offer maps so you can do a self-guided tour of the many historic buildings. All of these tours chronicle the lives of those visionary entrepreneurs who made this city what it is today, and you will marvel at the intricate details and architectural innovation put into every one of these magnificent buildings.

By taking one of these tours, you gain insight into how our city became what it is today.

Tulsa Foundation for Architecture
633 S. Boston Ave., Tulsa, OK 74119
(918) 583-5550, www.tulsaarchitecture.org/tours

Tulsa Historical Society
2445 S. Peoria Ave., Tulsa, OK 74114
(918) 712-9484, www.tulsahistory.org

Tours of Tulsa
(918) 625-4909, www.toursoftulsa.com

51

EXPERIENCE AN INTIMATE CONCERT

AT THE HISTORIC CAIN'S BALLROOM

Founded in 1923, this historic venue has been providing Tulsa everything from ballroom dancing lessons to musicals and concerts throughout the decades. It's affectionately known as "The House that Bob Built," a reference to the famous Western swing musician Bob Wills, who headlined with his band the Texas Playboys on the stage of Cain's Ballroom.

Cain's Ballroom is a one-room auditorium with a dome ceiling, a large bar, a concession area, and an upper VIP lounge. Large vintage photographs of iconic performers like Bob Wills, Hank Williams, Johnnie Lee Wills, Kay Starr, and others hang on the walls above the auditorium. They watch over the crowd at each show and remind us of the historical importance of this amazing venue.

Attending a show at the Cain's Ballroom is an experience. The standing-room-only policy makes it easy to get up close and personal with the talent, making it the one of the most intimate concert venues around. See you at the show!

423 N. Main St., Tulsa, OK 74103
(918) 584-2306, www.cainsballroom.com

GET A DOSE OF LAUGHTER

AT THE LOONY BIN COMEDY CLUB

There is scientific proof that laughter is the best medicine for your body and your soul. Laughter releases chemicals in your body that relieve stress, soothe tension, improve mood, help with pain, and boost your immune system.

The Tulsa Loony Bin is a good place to look for healing laughter. It is the city's only comedy club featuring local and touring professional stand-up comedians in a fun, lively setting. Join some friends for an evening of good food, tasty libations, and the healing power of laughter.

And if you happened to miss your calling as a comedian, participate in one of their open mic nights where you can show others why you are often a hit at a holiday party or get-together with family and friends.

6808 S. Memorial Dr., Ste. 234, Tulsa, OK 74133
(918) 392-5653, www.tulsa.loonybincomedy.com
www.facebook.com/LoonyBinTulsa

Open Wednesday–Saturday
Check local website or Facebook for the current calendar of events.

CHEER ON
THE TULSA TOUGH CYCLING COMPETITION

A big annual tradition here is the Saint Francis Tulsa Tough cycling competition, a three-day bicycle festival run throughout the Blue Dome, Tulsa Arts, and Riverside Districts. Sponsored by Saint Francis Hospital, this race has been entertaining and exciting residents since 2005 and occurs every year on the second weekend in June.

Professional and amateur racers from all over the country come to T-town for this high-stakes race through some of the most scenic routes in our city. Spectators fill the streets to watch bikes zip past at astonishing speeds vying for that prize.

The end of the race includes what is called "Cry Baby Hill." It is a grueling uphill route where people line the streets to cheer on the racers. Some people dress in costumes and some are chugging beer, and this part of the event turns it into one of the largest annual parties in the city. It's something to see!

To watch the Tulsa Tough race is a great experience for anyone at any age. Definitely put it and Cry Baby Hill on your bucket list!

St. Francis Tulsa Tough Competition
www.tulsatough.com

54

JOIN IN THE *ROCKY HORROR* FUN AT THE CIRCLE CINEMA

Built in 1928, the Circle Cinema is the oldest standing movie house in Tulsa. Today the cinema shows independent, foreign, and documentary films that you can't find anywhere else in town. They also have plays, silent films, classics, and limited release films like *The Rocky Horror Picture Show*.

The Rocky Horror Picture Show is an unusual comedy/musical/horror film created in 1975 based on a 1973 musical stage production of the same name. Only a few theaters will show it, and when they do it's a party.

Before entering the theater, you are given a paper sack with props to help you get into the spirit of the movie. You are encouraged to talk back to the screen and use the props in any way you see fit for an interactive movie experience like no other!

The showings are limited and usually only offered once a year during the last week of December. If you decide to go, be sure to let them know in the beginning if you've never seen it before.

10 S. Lewis Ave., Tulsa, OK 74104
(918) 585-3504, (918) 592-FILM (3456) for showtimes
www.circlecinema.org

TAKE A SELFIE ON LOCATION
OF *THE OUTSIDERS* MOVIE

One of the most famous films shot in Tulsa was *The Outsiders*, created in 1983 and based on the S. E. Hinton novel. The movie is about two rival gangs, the Greasers and Socs (Socials), in Tulsa during the 1960s. It depicts the rivalry, social division, and teen angst between the two groups.

Being a lifelong fan of the movie and novel, hip hop artist Danny Boy O'Connor purchased the Curtis Brothers (Greasers) house in 2016 and saved its history.

The old house is open by appointment for tours where you can step inside and see it just as it was in the movie. Additionally, you can sign up to take a tour of the *Outsiders* filming locations around the city and hear interesting facts about the movie-making process.

Get in touch with the museum and make your reservation to see a part of Tulsa film history!

The Outsiders House Museum
731 N. Saint Louis Ave., Tulsa, OK 74106
www.theoutsidershouse.com
www.facebook.com/theoutsidershouse

FEEL THE LAID-BACK VIBE
OF THE PEARL DISTRICT

The Pearl District is located on the east side of downtown and outside of the Inner Dispersal Loop. During the twentieth century, this urban neighborhood contained a lot of large manufacturing plants mixed in with tiny bungalow houses, grocery stores, and other shops for the needs of the nearby workers.

The decline in oil prices also took a toll on the manufacturing plants in the district, and much of this area was abandoned and neglected until a revitalization project turned it into a thriving neighborhood rich in possibility. Today it contains a park, several restored historic buildings, restaurants, breweries, a popular beauty parlor, and much more. It was designed so that people would have a walkable place to work and play.

The pull of the Pearl District is its laid-back charm. Quaint shops and cozy restaurants make this area a hidden gem. Plan to spend an entire day exploring all that the Pearl District has to offer.

Pearl District Association of Tulsa, OK
www.tulsapearl.org

BE READY FOR ANYTHING
AT THE EXPO SQUARE

The Tulsa Expo Square is a large facility off 21st Street on the Fairgrounds. It was constructed in 1931 and holds many special events throughout the year.

Everything from gun and knife shows, car shows, and monster truck events, to wedding shows, flea markets, and more can be experienced at the Tulsa Expo Square. A very popular event called Just Between Friends takes place there and is the largest children's and maternity consignment sales event in the city. The large plot of land offers plenty of parking and easy facility access. A variety of concession stands are available to quench your thirst or fill your rumbling tummy during these events.

There is much to do and see during any given month at the Expo Square. Visit their website for a current calendar of events.

Expo Square, Tulsa Fairgrounds
4145 E. 21st St., Tulsa, OK 74114
(918) 744-1113, www.exposquare.com

IT'S GAME ON!
AT SHUFFLES

Located in the historic Archer building downtown is a fairly new addition to the arts district and fun little place called Shuffles. This board game café has every game you can imagine, and not only offers table rentals but also drinks, coffee, food, and more.

This restaurant, bar, and coffee shop is a great place to gather with friends, choose a board game off the shelf (if you can decide which one from their massive library!), and enjoy a favorite old pastime. Put down your phones because these games require your undivided attention.

It's a good idea to rent a table with small drink holders in the side so as not to interfere with your table game. Shuffles hosts karaoke, trivia nights, and other events that allow you to sit back and enjoy a friendly-but-competitive board game while sipping a hot cup of joe, delicious food, or a beer or craft cocktail with friends and family.

Shuffles Board Game Café
207 E. Archer St. Unit #E, Tulsa, OK 74103
(918) 728-7252, www.shufflestulsa.com

59

CHECK OUT THE SHARK EXHIBIT
AT THE OKLAHOMA AQUARIUM

The Oklahoma Aquarium is in the suburb of Jenks. This 72,000 square-foot facility brings you over a hundred exhibits and thousands of aquatic animals and water-related culture to explore. With hands-on activities from petting stingrays to watching members of the biology staff feed the dangerous bull sharks, there is something new to learn around almost every corner.

One of the most unique opportunities offered at the aquarium is a tunnel that allows patrons to walk safe and dry through the 380,000-gallon saltwater shark tank which contains twenty of the largest bull sharks kept in activity. This dimly lit tunnel has you surrounded by some of the most dangerous sharks known to man.

The sharks swim all around you as you walk through the tunnel and get up close and personal with this intriguing species. You can also get the best seats in the house to witness feeding times by checking the aquarium's website.

Visit the Oklahoma aquarium to get acquainted with all your favorite furry, finned, feathered, flippered, and fun oceanic creatures.

300 Aquarium Dr., Jenks, OK 74037
(918) 296-3474, www.okaquarium.org

60

PLAY AROUND
AT TULSA'S ENTERTAINMENT CENTERS

Tulsa is an entertainment city and we have our fair share of places offering a myriad of things to do under one roof. These one-stop entertainment centers offer bowling, video games, great food, live shows, and much more, making it easy to get the family together for a fun night out.

Although some are chains, Tulsa boasts a few of her own like The Max Retropub and Andy B's Tulsa. Each of these locally owned game venues offers unique décor and a themed environment for your gaming pleasure.

For a fun evening out and lots to do under one roof, check out these places in Tulsa.

The Max Retropub
114 S. Elgin Ave., Tulsa, OK 74120
(918) 895-6200, www.maxretropub.com

Main Event
7830 S. Santa Fe Ave. W., Tulsa, OK 74132
(918) 447-1200, www.mainevent.com

Cinergy Entertainment Group
6808 S. Memorial Dr., Ste. 300, Tulsa, OK 74133
(918) 894-6888, www.cinergy.com/locations/tulsa

Dave & Buster's
6812 S. 105th E. Ave., Tulsa, OK 74133
(918) 449-3100, www.daveandbusters.com/locations/tulsa

Andy B's Tulsa
8711 S. Lewis Ave., Tulsa, OK 74137
(918) 299-9494, www.bowlandybs.com/location/tulsaok

Tulsa's Incredible Pizza Company
8314 E. 71st St., Tulsa, OK 74133
(539) 302-2681, www.incrediblepizza.com/tulsa

CELEBRATE "PASSED" LIVES

AT THE DAY OF THE DEAD FESTIVAL

Every year on November first and second, immediately after Halloween, the Living Arts of Tulsa puts on a festival to honor loved ones who have passed away. The official name of this celebration is *Día de Los Muertos*, meaning Day of the Dead, and it is a Hispanic holiday that celebrates ancestors and heritage with altars, music, decorations, dancing, and singing. This Mexican and Central American tradition fuses together the Roman Catholic holidays of All Saints and All Souls Days.

The Living Arts of Tulsa accepts applications year-round, and anyone whose application is accepted is allowed to set up an altar to represent their family and heritage. The outdoor festival is held in the Greenwood District on the south block of East Reconciliation Way and North Detroit Ave., with merchandise tents and food trucks available, so be sure to check it out and be mesmerized by all the candles, altars, and spiritual connections honoring the loved ones who've passed.

Living Arts Tulsa
307 E. Reconciliation Way, Tulsa, OK 74120
(918) 585-1234, www.livingarts.org

TIP
Day of the Dead Festival, November 1,
5:00 p.m.–11:00 p.m. Altars are kept up on
display until around November 22nd.

62

DRESS RAD FOR THE '80S PROM
AT THE HISTORIC CAIN'S BALLROOM

Ahhh, the '80s! The decade of Aquanet hairspray and gaudy bright neon colors; who wouldn't want to relive it?

Every year Cain's Ballroom is the location of the '80s Prom where you can dress up, show up, and enjoy the bygone era of big hair and big hopes. The prom has been in existence longer than the decade itself. Participants put on elaborate costumes depicting the era and come dressed as toys, bands, pop icons, movie characters, and more. The two people in the best costumes are crowned Prom King and Prom Queen during the event.

The DJ will spin your favorite '80s tunes as you dance the night away watching old commercials, cartoons, and popular icons on massive projection screens. Engage in hilarious and clever stage skits performing scenes from popular '80s movies like *Ghostbusters*, *Goonies*, and *Dirty Dancing*. Enjoy an '80s fashion show and more!

Organize a group of friends, don some lurid and loud costumes, and have a rad evening! Trust me, it's like, totally awesome!

423 N. Main St., Tulsa, OK 74103
(918) 584-2306, www.80sprom.com

TIP

Guests who purchase a VIP ticket will be treated to exclusive access to the mezzanine area for fun extras like decade-themed snacks, complimentary photo booth tickets and an overhead view of one totally rad party.

The ’80s

Rubik’s Cube launched at the International Toy Fair

Pac Man video game is released

Who shot JR?

RIP John Lennon

MTV debuts

The wreckage of the Titanic was found

The Berlin Wall came down

The Simpsons first seen on Tracy Ullman show

Michael Jackson released Thriller album

63

HANG OUT WITH THE BEST LOCAL TALENT
AT THE HUNT CLUB

The live music scene in Tulsa is an exceptional one, and Tulsa has a lot of talent to showcase in local venues. One of the few pubs that still offers the opportunity to drop in and hear a local band is located right in the downtown arts district.

On the corner of Cameron and Main Streets in downtown Tulsa is The Hunt Club. As the name suggests, the club sports a hunting theme of stuffed bears, raccoons, and other trophies as its signature décor along with fine wood tables, comfortable booths, delicious food, an outside terrace, and outdoor rooftop seating with a spectacular view of the Tulsa skyline.

For the past decade, The Hunt Club has given local artists and musicians a place to show off their musical talent and has allowed the patrons the chance to enjoy a cold beverage, yummy food, and great tunes in a casual setting.

So the next time you are out and about in downtown Tulsa, stop by The Hunt Club to enjoy some local music and fun.

224 N. Main St., Tulsa, OK 74103
(918) 599-9200, www.thehuntclubtulsa.com

TAKE IN A PLAY OR A CONCERT

AT THE HISTORIC TULSA MUNICIPAL THEATER

Formerly known as the Brady Theater, this gem of a venue has been bringing some big names to Tulsa since 1914. Legends like Mae West, Audrey Hepburn, and Will Rogers have graced the stage of the old theater, and mid-twentieth-century greats like Willie Nelson, Cindy Lauper, and Alice Cooper have also performed there. Pretty much every genre of music and every one of the performing arts have enthralled audiences on the theater's large stage.

Today, the theater continues to host acts from all over the world. Iconic photos of legendary performers adorn the walls which, combined with the wonderful acoustics and intimate vibe, provide an impressive historic ambiance that sets the tone for your entertainment experience.

One step inside and it's easy to see why this historical venue is one of the most famous theaters in all of Oklahoma.

105 Reconciliation Way, Tulsa, OK 74103
(918) 582-7239, (800) 514-3849 for tickets
www.bradytheater.com

ONEOK FIELD
HOME OF THE TULSA DRILLERS

SPORTS AND RECREATION

65

INDULGE YOUR SENSE OF ADVENTURE
AT THE GATHERING PLACE

The recently built sixty-six-acre green space known as the Gathering Place was a generous gift from the philanthropist and Tulsa advocate George B. Kaiser. It includes a sports complex, a BMX track, a skatepark, a concert venue, playgrounds, trails, gardens, restaurants, and so much more.

Located on Tulsa's riverfront property, the Gathering Place provides an impressive lineup of inviting activities to spark your sense of adventure. Known as "the park for everyone," there is no entry fee and almost all activities are free as well. You can sit quietly on a deck and enjoy the Tulsa skyline, or rent a kayak, canoe, or paddleboat and explore the creek that runs through the park. This park has it all.

The Gathering Place won awards before it had even been open a full year. It was named "Best New Attraction in the United States" by *USA Today* in 2018 and was included in the "100 Greatest Places of 2019" list by *Time* magazine.

Make your way and explore one of the coolest attractions that Tulsa has to offer.

2650 S. John Williams Way E., Tulsa, OK 74114
(918) 779-1000, www.gatheringplace.org

GET SWALLOWED BY A BLUE WHALE
IN CATOOSA

The Blue Whale is an old roadside attraction in the suburbs of Catoosa, Oklahoma. Built by Hugh Davis in 1979, this eighty-foot-long whale was a gift for his wife on their anniversary and sat next to a spring-fed pond on their property. Although it was intended only for private use, it quickly became the favorite swimming spot for neighboring kids. Davis eventually opened it up to the public and added a trading post, a large replica of Noah's Ark, and an animal reptile kingdom to make it a park, calling it Nature's Acres.

It closed when the family retired in the late '80s. The pond eventually got scummy, the ark and the whale fell into disrepair, and the park was abandoned, but remains a favorite stop for travelers on iconic Route 66.

Although you can't swim there anymore, the Blue Whale continues to get hundreds of visitors each year. Local booster groups help maintain the old whale so that visitors can enjoy a nostalgic trip down memory lane.

Blue Whale—Catoosa
2600 N. Oklahoma 66 (Rt. 66), Catoosa, OK 74105

CHEER FOR THE DRILLERS
AT ONEOK FIELD

Located in the historic Greenwood District, the ONEOK baseball field is home to the Tulsa Drillers, our minor league baseball team. During the spring and summer months fans can attend an exciting game of baseball while sitting comfortably in the stands to enjoy America's favorite pastime.

Enjoy some peanuts and Cracker Jack or grab a cold beer and a corn dog. Every type of stadium food or drink is on offer for your pleasure and readily available.

ONEOK Field hosts All-Star games and has the most amazing fireworks shows. After any home game on a Friday night, the stadium puts on an incredible firework display visible to anyone near the downtown area, but especially awesome to those in the stands sitting directly underneath them.

These family-friendly events change with the schedule so be sure to check their website for game schedules and times. Membership packages are available which give you lots of extra opportunities to be a part of the action during the baseball season.

Tulsa Drillers Baseball, ONEOK Field
201 N. Elgin Ave., Tulsa, OK 74120
(918) 744-5998, www.milb.com/tulsa

CRUISE
RIVERSIDE DRIVE

There is a long stretch of riverfront property featuring long intertwining trails through nicely paved and manicured pathways. Biking and walking trails, shops, restaurants, and entertainment amenities can all be found in this area known as Riverside Drive. It stretches from 11th Street to 101st Street and gives you virtually miles of places to see and things to do.

A variety of locally-owned bars and grills will keep you refreshed with delicious food and drinks, while the River West Festival Park will keep you entertained with fun events like Oktoberfest, The Color Run, and the annual *Cinco de Mayo* festival.

Or if you are looking for some action, you can join in some long-standing Tulsa traditions like the Tulsa Polar Plunge or the Great River Raft Race. There is never a shortage of things to do on the riverfront.

RiverParks Authority
2424 E. 21st St., Ste. 300, Tulsa, OK 74114
(918) 596-2001, www.riverparks.org

HIKE THE URBAN WILDERNESS OF TURKEY MOUNTAIN

Turkey Mountain is an urban wilderness set in the heart of our beautiful city. From beginner-level trails to deep, steep ravines for the more experienced hiker, there is a lot of rugged terrain to explore.

Located on the west side of Tulsa with easy access off South Elwood Avenue at 67th Street, Turkey Mountain occupies over three hundred acres. It is covered with tall trees, brush, ponds, and large boulders, creating a landscape that makes you forget you are actually still within city limits.

It's a great way to spend the day, but be sure to wear appropriate clothing and shoes. This land is undeveloped and contains large tree roots, rough rock, and trails labeled by color to indicate difficulty level. Lose yourself in the woods. You can literally get lost for hours at Turkey Mountain and spend time with Mother Nature to clear your soul, right here in Tulsa.

Turkey Mountain Wilderness, run by RiverParks Authority
2424 E. 21st St., Ste. 300, Tulsa, OK 74114
(918) 596-2001, www.riverparks.org/turkey-mountain-project

CHOOSE YOUR FAVORITE
CITY PARK

The parks and recreation department oversees 135 parks throughout the city, making Tulsa even more inviting and welcoming. Some of the parks are nature preserves, while others host fitness facilities, skate parks, swimming pools, playgrounds, sports complexes, picnic areas, and golf courses.

One of the more popular parks is LaFortune, which is well known for its golf course and five-mile walking path. Haikey Creek Park is in demand for its creekside wilderness trail. Hunter Park is frequented by dog lovers because it contains a dog park for their fur babies, and Chandler Park has lots of hidden rock formations perfect for rock-climbing and hiking. Chandler also boasts a baseball complex, two disc golf courses, and the largest splash park in Oklahoma. One of the more picturesque public areas is Woodward Park, which has botanical garden backdrops that make it a popular hot spot for photographers.

Whichever outdoor activity appeals to you on a given day, there is a unique park in the Tulsa area that has everything you need.

71

PLAN A STAYCATION
AT A LOCAL RESORT

Sometimes you need to get away from the same old familiar routine. In Tulsa, recharging your batteries and renewing your soul can be accomplished in close proximity to the city. Escape to a wooded wilderness or even a local boutique hotel to treat yourself to a weekend of rest and relaxation. The best part is that you don't have to drive a great distance or spend a lot of money on airfare with so many great local options for helping you de-stress.

Tulsa is home to a few local resorts where you can unwind and be pampered in a secluded getaway. Explore nature in neighboring suburbs and towns as a way to reduce your tension and disconnect from everyday stresses.

Schedule a day or a weekend away at one of these local resorts to treat your body, mind, and soul to a much-needed break.

Post Oak Lodge & Retreat
5323 W. 31st St. N., Tulsa, OK 74127
(918) 425-2112, www.postoaklodge.com

River Spirit Casino & Resort
8330 Riverside Pkwy., Tulsa, OK 74137
www.riverspirittulsa.com

Skelly Lodge
27795 S. Skelly Rd., Catoosa, OK 74015
(918) 770-6090, www.skellylodge.com

Cedar Rock Inn
4501 W. 41st St., Tulsa, OK 74107
(918) 447-4493, www.cedarrockinn.com

SCAN THE CITY LIGHTS
FROM CHANDLER PARK

One of the hidden treasures in Tulsa is Chandler Park with its amazing hilltop views. It is located across the Arkansas River on West 21st Street. Perched on a hilltop in the middle of the small thriving industrial community of Berryhill, the high altitude of the park makes for some of the best panoramic views in Tulsa.

The vista from the top of the ridge at sunset on a nice evening seems like a divine gift. Once the sun sets, you get incredible views of the city lights in downtown Tulsa and Sand Springs.

Chandler Park is also home to Lights on the Hill, an impressive display of holiday lights set throughout the park during the Christmas season.

Whether it is natural or man-made lights you are going to see, Chandler Park is the place to go for spectacular views from atop the hill. Pack a blanket and maybe a picnic basket for a chance to watch the sunset or the city lights in a peaceful setting.

6500 W. 21st St., Tulsa, OK 74107

PAINT THE WILDLIFE
AT OXLEY NATURE CENTER

This nature center near Mohawk Park and Tulsa Zoo is nestled away in an area of dense trees and provides several walking trails and a plethora of Oklahoma wildlife. There are 804 acres in this native sanctuary known as the Oxley Nature Center.

This preserved space is a place to get away from the sounds of the city and forget you are still within its limits. Experience a deep connection with nature and participate in some of the many interactive programs they have available. Oxley offers everything from bird and butterfly walks and specified wildlife viewing areas to drawing and painting classes.

Managed as part of the Oxley Center, the Redbud Valley Nature Preserve is a space that will please your senses and get you in tune with nature. Its mission is to preserve the plants and animals that are native to the valley. Sit, relax, turn off your phone and electronic devices, admire the view, and soak in all that is natural on this earth.

6700 Mohawk Blvd., Tulsa, OK 74115
(918) 596-9054

74

LEARN THE TRAGIC SECRET BEHIND TULSA'S OLDEST HOUSE

On a corner in Owen Park sits a one-room, side-gabled house built in the 1800s which predates the land rush. What used to be the home of preacher and philanthropist Sylvester Morris is Tulsa's oldest home still standing today.

Reverend Morris was a preacher who started several churches in the Tulsa area, but his life was cut short when he was mistaken for a bootlegger and killed by lawmen. Although his home is memorialized because of its age, it is fitting that we should also be reminded of this tragic accidental death and continue to honor his name to this day.

As a historic landmark, the house serves as a reminder of what life was like back in the 1800s. Stop by and see a part of Tulsa's past in this well-preserved old homestead.

Owen Park
560 N. Maybelle Ave., Tulsa, OK 74127

PAY YOUR RESPECTS
AT JOHN HOPE FRANKLIN RECONCILIATION PARK

Located in the historic Greenwood District in Tulsa is a place where our past and present unite to tell important stories from Oklahoma's history.

The park was built in 2008 with city, state, and private funding as a reminder of how prosperous and forgiving the black community has been here in Tulsa. The park conducts tours that highlight the 1921 Race Massacre, Black Wall Street, Native and African American immigration, and other educational information connected to historic Greenwood.

The park is a symbol of hope. It is a memorial to the person it's named after and also a reminder of one of the darkest parts of Tulsa history. Take time to reflect, pray, and aspire to a new time of reconciliation.

321 N. Detroit Ave., Tulsa, OK 74103
(918) 295-5009

TAKE TIME OUT

FOR A TULSA OILERS HOCKEY GAME

One of the minor league franchises that Tulsa supports is the Tulsa Oilers hockey team. An evening or afternoon spent watching an intense game of hockey can make for a fun family outing.

The hockey team was originally started in the late 1920s but gained even more popularity in the early 1990s. The Oilers have been winning games for a long time and have given Tulsa fans many a sweet taste of hometown victory.

The team's season runs October through April, and you can purchase a single ticket to any game or a pass for the whole season. The games are held at the BOK Center and offer a fast-paced, riveting night of sports competition on the ice and friendly rivalry in the stands.

Full amenities are available along with all the concessions your heart could desire. If you're lucky you might even have a chance to get up close and personal with the players for selfies and autographs after the game.

Tulsa Oilers Hockey
www.tulsaoilers.com

BOK Center
200 S. Denver Ave., Tulsa, OK 74103

77

SWIM UP FOR A DRINK AT THE POOLBAR

AT RIVER SPIRIT CASINO

River Spirit Casino and Resort offers something different for summer fun in Tulsa at their outdoor pool. There you will find a full-service swim-up bar, palm trees, soothing colors, and private cabanas to rent as you are expertly served and pampered like a celebrity.

The Landshark Poolbar at the River Spirit Casino is like no other. Nowhere else in Tulsa can you watch a show on the bar's TV and never leave the pool! They even have tables in the pool to keep your drink in check while you soak up the sun.

The pool is open from 10:00 a.m. until dusk and has separate adult and kid sections. Day passes are available for a small fee if you are not a hotel guest.

This is truly poolside relaxation at its best. The pool is open seasonally and provides a unique, fun way to spend a hot, sweltering summer day.

Landshark Poolbar at River Spirit Casino & Resort
8330 Riverside Pkwy., Tulsa, OK 74137
(888) 748-3731

CHEER ON THE HURRICANE
AT A TU FOOTBALL GAME

The Tulsa Golden Hurricane is the college football team for the University of Tulsa in the NCAA division. Games are held at Skelly Field at H. A. Chapman football stadium located around 11th Street and Harvard Avenue.

The stadium was originally constructed in 1930 and was named Skelly Field but was later changed to Skelly Stadium. It was changed again in 2007 and in keeping with nostalgia, it is now Skelly Field at H. A. Chapman Stadium. The arena seats thirty thousand and has concession stands, restrooms, a luxury box, and club level seating.

Redeem your ticket, grab some food and drinks from the concession stands, and enjoy some of the best live entertainment Tulsa has to offer. Nothing gives you a sense of pride and community quite like a TU Football game. Join others from near and far to witness the players battle it out for rankings.

Located at the University of Tulsa
3112 E. 8th St., Tulsa, OK 74104
www.tulsahurricane.com

FIND YOUR BLISS WITH YOGA

AT GUTHRIE GREEN

Yoga is a mental, spiritual and physical practice composed of stretching, breathing, and somatic poses. It's an ancient Hindu practice that has been around for thousands of years and strengthens a direct connection between mind, body and spirit. It's good practice for the physique and a good practice for the soul.

As part of a wellness initiative sponsored by the city of Tulsa, anyone can attend free outdoor yoga classes at Guthrie Green downtown throughout the spring, summer, and fall. Generally offered on Monday and Wednesday evenings at 5:30 p.m., classes are taught by trained instructors who demonstrate different yoga techniques to interested participants on the lawn, weather permitting. These classes are part of Fitness on the Green, an outdoor program designed to cater to the curious and the health conscious. They are totally free and anyone at any skill level is welcome to participate.

So bring your yoga mat and meet with others on the Guthrie Green lawn for a free one-hour yoga class and watch it transform your life.

Fitness on the Green, Guthrie Green
111 E. Reconciliation Way, Tulsa, OK 74103
www.guthriegreen.com/events/fitness-on-the-green-yoga

GET YOUR FRUSTRATIONS OUT
WITH URBAN AX THROWING

The Canadian pastime of ax throwing has come to America and is all the rage. This sport has been around for centuries, but is just now gaining popularity in modern American culture.

While it may sound dangerous, it's actually not. Ax-throwing facilities are opening up all over the city and provide a diverting, safe, and unique outing. Even better, leagues are forming so that skilled throwers can compete all over the country and show off their newly acquired abilities.

Participants line up to throw an ax as hard as they can at a wooden target with a bullseye and various colored lines and spaces to aim at for points. Most places have an ax-throwing coach to help beginners and the throwing cages are generally located indoors which makes it a great competitive activity any time of year.

Try your hand at ax throwing and free your inner lumberjack. Be sure to wear comfortable clothes and book your time slot to see what all the excitement is about.

Got Wood Ax Throwing
103 E. Main St., Jenks, OK 74037
(918) 528-3303, www.gotwoodaxethrowing.com

Angry Ax
7 N. Peoria Ave., Tulsa, OK 74120
(918) 917-9015, www.angryaxe.com

A&R Ax Throwing
6975 S. Lewis Ave., Tulsa, OK 74136
(918) 764-8808, www.aandraxes.com

STOP AND SMELL THE ROSES

AT TULSA GARDEN CENTER

Designed by architect Noble B. Fleming in 1919 and built for oil magnate David R. Travis, this gorgeous Italian-style villa now known as the Tulsa Garden Center has twenty-one rooms and ten bathrooms. It cost a whopping hundred thousand dollars to build, which may not seem like a lot of money today, but back then must have made it downright swanky.

The mansion has changed ownership several times and was gifted to the city of Tulsa by W. G. Skelly in 1954. He envisioned a place for horticultural education and that is what we have today. The Linnaeus Teaching Garden on the property, an extensive library, and rose gardens make it a horticulture heaven.

One thing is for sure: the history of the old mansion and its amazing architecture will surprise and delight you. Once you have absorbed all that, it will seem natural to find a bench along one of the many garden paths, take a seat, and enjoy the view. Don't forget to smell the roses!

2435 S. Peoria Ave., Tulsa, OK 74114
(918) 576-5155

The gardens next to Woodward Park,
and the park itself, have curfews,
so be sure to check for signs!

Garden Center Mansion Hours:
Tuesday–Friday 9:00 a.m.–4:00 p.m.
Closed Saturdays for private events
Closed to the public on Sunday and Monday

82

LUXURIATE
AT THE LAKE

Luckily, Tulsa is surrounded by lakes that can take you away from the hustle and bustle of city life. Several of our area lakes offer campgrounds, RV hookups, canoe and float rentals, food and drink concessions, grills, and much more. You can rent a site and spend the weekend in a natural setting and indulge in the peace to solitude of your own little space.

Natural beauty will surround you at these popular lakes and you can fish, boat, swim, and camp to your heart's content. The area lakes have walking trails, natural waterfalls, rope swings, playgrounds, and so much to offer that you will have enough to do and see to fill up an entire weekend. Some places require permits for fishing and boating, so be sure to check ahead of time.

Listed here are a few lakes closest to the Tulsa area.

Skiatook Lake
5353 Lake Rd., Skiatook, OK 74070
(918) 396-3170

Lake Eufaula
111563 Hwy. 150, Checotah, OK 74426
(918) 689-5311

Lake Yahola
5701 E. 36th St. N., Tulsa, OK 74115
(918) 596-2100

Lake Bixhoma
18019 S. 161st E. Ave., Bixby, OK 74008

Keystone Lake
1926 Highway 151, Sand Springs, OK 74063

83

RAISE FUNDS AND HEART RATES

FOR CHARITY IN A CITY-SPONSORED RACE

The city of Tulsa regularly sponsors races for runners of all ages and skill levels. If you are not a runner, you can jog or walk, but any way you do it, competing in a race leaves you with a sense of exhilarating fulfillment.

We have the Golden Driller Marathon, the Jingle Bell Run, the Wicked Wine Run, and the Color Run, just to name a few. Many of them offer 1K and 5K options which is good for both the novice and the experienced runner. Several have fun themes to keep the momentum going and generate enthusiasm, and these make for a truly awesome experience. Many of these runs are for charity as well, which means you would be participating to support a worthy cause.

If you dare to enter, a race is an exciting event to be a part of and gives you a sense of community, wellness, and personal satisfaction. Find a run that supports a cause you are interested in and sign up!

TIP

Visit www.runningintheusa.com and look up Tulsa county for more information on a variety of upcoming races and events.

84

BE OFF TO THE RACES
AT FAIR MEADOWS

Fair Meadows is the place in Tulsa to see live horse races and watch the national races with other fans on a big screen. This sport has been around since 4500 BC and gets even more recognition during famous races like the Kentucky Derby and Preakness Stakes.

Watch as prized thoroughbreds race to compete for the cup, and if you go for the showing of a famous race like the Kentucky Derby, don't forget your hat! During those races they also have giveaways, promotions, and special drawings to help you get into the festivities.

Take a seat in the stands and feel the rush as pounding hooves hit the dirt and jockeys vie to push their horses to the finish line and the ultimate prize. Attending a race is free, but you have to be eighteen or older to place bets on the horses. It's a thrilling pastime to watch these powerful animals thunder around the track and to bet on your favorite underdog or the horse with the most unique name.

Check the website for live events and enjoy the food, drinks, and excitement of horse racing.

4705 E. 21st St., Tulsa, OK 74114
(918) 744-1113, www.exposquare.com/fairmeadows

CULTURE AND HISTORY

REFINE YOUR CULTURE
AT TULSA'S FINEST MUSEUMS

Tulsa is home of many exquisite museums that celebrate everything to do with fine art, history, and culture.

The Gilcrease Museum has one of the world's largest collections of Native American art and includes the Helmerich Center for American Research, a library and archive of maps, rare books, photographs, and manuscripts. The Philbrook Museum is another favorite located in the former mansion of the rich oilman Waite Phillips and his wife Genevieve. It houses the most amazing collection of modern and contemporary art that Tulsa has to offer. The Tulsa Historical Society and Museum is located in the old Travis mansion built around 1919. It contains a little bit of everything connected with Tulsa and her past. Rotating exhibits and exciting artifact collections directly related to Tulsa's history can be found there.

Take an afternoon to enjoy the gardens, art, culture, or architecture of one of these local museums, then take some more time to plan your visit to the next one on the list until you've seen them all.

Gilcrease Museum

1400 N. Gilcrease Museum Rd., Tulsa, OK 74127

(918) 596-2700

Philbrook Museum

2727 S. Rockford Rd., Tulsa, OK 74114

(918) 748-5300

Tulsa Historical Society

2445 S. Peoria Ave., Tulsa, OK 74114

(918) 712-9484

86

MARVEL AT THE SIZE
OF THE TULSA DRILLER

The *Golden Driller* is such an iconic treasure in Tulsa that it was adopted by the Oklahoma legislature as the state monument in 1979. It is located in front of the Expo Square buildings on the north side of 21st Street between Yale and Harvard.

This seventy-five-foot tall statue of an oil worker was erected in 1959 for the International Petroleum Exposition and stands proudly in front of the Expo Square building. It's the sixth-tallest free-standing statue in the United States and weighs over 43,500 pounds. It is a reminder of the hard-working oilmen who made a better life for all Tulsans with the discovery of oil.

Today the large figure is a roadside tourist attraction and symbolic icon for our city and state. An authentic oil derrick was taken from a depleted oil field in Seminole, Oklahoma, and stands next to him as he lays his forearm and hand casually across the top. He is a reminder of Tulsa's glory days when we were the Oil Capital of the World and a major player on the national stage.

Golden Driller Statue
4145 E. 21st St., Tulsa, OK 74114

87

DRIVE BY
THE 220+ YEAR-OLD BUR OAK HANGING TREE

Many Tulsans are unaware that we still have a hanging tree here in Tulsa. Located in a fenced lot on North Lawton Avenue in downtown Tulsa, this very old bur oak tree has outlived many people and events throughout the decades. Local legends suggest that between fifteen and twenty people were hung from the twelve-foot hanging branch for violating Creek Indian law between 1870 and 1889.

While standing next to or sitting under this majestic tree, one thing is certain: if this old and historic living landmark could talk, it would have some hair-raising stories to tell.

Today, it graces the parking lot of the Oktoberfest warehouse, gated up at night, but during the day you can picnic under the tree if you so desire. A picnic table sits next to its enormous trunk and you can take advantage of its generous shade while you speculate on the many historical events that have occurred during its long lifetime.

3 N. Lawton Ave., Tulsa, OK 74127

88

LIFT UP YOUR HEART
WITH THE PRAYING HANDS

One of the first things my mother took me to see when we moved to Tulsa was the *Praying Hands* sculpture at Oral Roberts University. Back then, they were located in front of the City of Faith Medical and Research Center at 81st Street and Lewis Avenue and were called *The Healing Hands*. This amazing bronze sculpture is the largest of its kind in the world, standing sixty feet tall and weighing thirty tons. It's truly an impressive art installation to see up close.

The City of Faith Medical and Research Center was a faith-based healing center that Oral Roberts said he was ordered to build when a 640-foot Jesus appeared to him in a dream. Due to numerous lawsuits, the City of Faith went bankrupt in 1989 and the hands were moved to the entrance of Oral Roberts University where they still stand today.

The praying hands welcome visitors to Oral Roberts University, reminding them of the religious doctrine that the school was founded upon, what the school is about . . . and always to pray.

Oral Roberts University
7777 S. Lewis Ave., Tulsa, OK 74136

CATCH A SHOW
AT TULSA LITTLE THEATER

Tulsa Little Theatre at 15th and Delaware Streets is a historical icon. Built in 1932, the structure with its underground stage was a small community theater with big hopes. Through several incarnations, the Little Theatre changed names from Theatre Tulsa to Delaware Playhouse and back to Tulsa Little Theatre again. In between all those changes, the theater has been a private residence and a venue for private parties and has survived two devastating fires. By the twenty-first century, the old building was worn and tired and had fallen into major disrepair.

The Tulsa Little Theatre was given new life when Bryce Hill, a local Tulsa attorney, purchased the old building in 2004. He saved the old structure, restoring it to its former glory, making it his law office, and renting out the theater space for concerts, musicals, plays, and private events.

If you're in the Cherry Street area, take a peek into the theater if it is open and check out the meticulous attention to detail the Hills put into restoring this little piece of Tulsa history.

Tulsa Little Theater, Law Offices of Bryce Hill
1511 S. Delaware Ave., Tulsa, OK 74104
(918) 749-0020, www.tulsalittletheatre.com

90

EXPERIENCE A NEW SPIRITUAL VIBE
AT THE TAM BAO BUDDHIST TEMPLE

Tam Bao is a Buddhist temple established in 1993 by Vietnamese refugees who had settled in Tulsa after the fall of Saigon in 1975. Pooling their money and resources, they were able to buy the five acres of land where the temple sits today.

Visitors to the temple grounds have called it beautiful, calming, and serene. Many like to take their problems to the majestic statues including a fifty-seven-foot, 400,000-pound granite statue of Kuan Yin. The statue was erected to remind visitors to embody the values of Kuan Yin, compassion and kindness.

The temple doors are open to anyone who wants to enter. Worshippers conduct big celebrations on Buddha's birthday when you are invited to "bathe the Buddha" to cleanse yourself of any attachments you've accumulated over the year.

The grounds are open from 8:00 a.m. until 9:00 p.m. and you are welcome to visit during those times, sit in meditation, and open yourself up to enlightenment.

16933 E. 21st St., Tulsa, OK 74134
(918) 438-0714

LEARN THE AMAZING HISTORY OF THE COUNCIL OAK TREE

When you think of Oklahoma, sometimes cowboys and Indians come to mind. Proof of the existence of a Native American presence in Tulsa is the Council Oak Tree, one of the historically significant landmarks of the Creek Indians who were marched to Oklahoma from Alabama in 1836.

After the government allotted them land in what was then called Indian Territory, they claimed a tree on a hill that overlooked the Arkansas River and built their village, naming it Talasi which translated as "Old Town." Talasi later became Tulsey Town and later just Tulsa.

The Council Oak Tree is on the National Register of Historic Places and was once the site of important ceremonies, council business, feasts, games, and tribal events.

The Park also includes a monument that represents the suffering the Creek endured during their trek on the "Trail of Tears."

Creek Nation Council Oak Park
1750 S. Cheyenne Ave., Tulsa, OK 74119

Hours:
Open daily from 7:00 a.m. to 10:00 p.m.

STIMULATE YOUR SENSES
AT AHHA TULSA

Founded as the Arts and Humanities Council of Tulsa, this interactive and sensory-art exploration museum is an experience like no other.

The Hardesty Center in the historic arts district was erected in 2012 and contains offices, classrooms, galleries, darkrooms, a printmaking suite, and studios for artists. This institution is one that will help cultivate the arts in Tulsa and develop programs that bring the arts to the public.

Different exhibits are offered, but *The Experience: Imagine* is one that seems to have people talking. It is a sensory-perceptive, totally immersive, multimedia experience which is the creation of six local artists. Sight, sound, movement, and touch will all be enthralled with this interactive exhibit that feels like a dream as it plays with your senses.

Be sure to check their website for the different classes and exhibits offered. They occasionally host artist talks and gallery events as well.

101 E. Archer St., Tulsa, OK 74103
(918) 584-3333, www.ahhatulsa.org

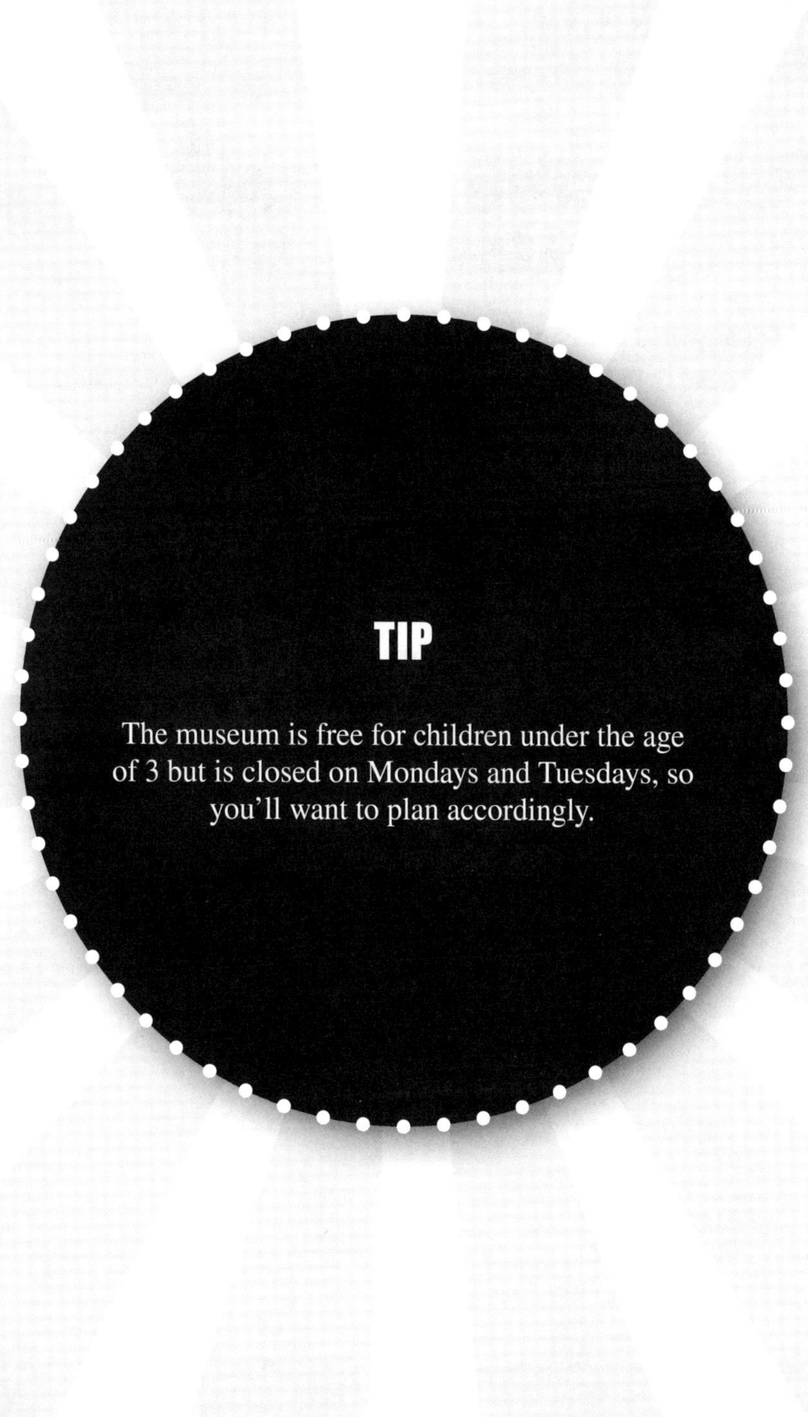

TIP

The museum is free for children under the age of 3 but is closed on Mondays and Tuesdays, so you'll want to plan accordingly.

93

SEE AND REMEMBER
BLACK WALL STREET

When you are visiting downtown Tulsa, be sure to put the Greenwood District on your agenda, not only for the historical nature of the district but also for the revitalization that makes it a must-see.

What was once the most prosperous African-American community in the United States (known as "Black Wall Street") was destroyed by fire during the 1921 race riots, but the resurgence of this vibrant area is a testament to the perseverance of this community. Plaques on the sidewalks tell of the places, people, and property that once thrived here and are remembered today.

Today, Greenwood is a reminder that hate may carry the battle but it does not always win the war. When you visit, you will find a revived business district that is a monument to Greenwood's checkered history as depicted in the spectacular mural adorning one of the Greenwood buildings, a reminder of how far we have yet to go, while still showing hope for the future.

Greenwood District
N. Greenwood Ave. at Archer St.

BE MESMERIZED
AT THE TULSA BALLET

Another time-honored tradition in Tulsa began in 1956 when two internationally known dancers and a professional musician created a place of artistic elegance. Today the Tulsa Ballet strives to maintain the excellence inspired by its founders, and it does not disappoint.

Located near the trendy Brookside district, the Tulsa Ballet offers world-class ballet performances regarded as some of the best in the United States. They also offer classes, community outreach programs, and productions that receive international acclaim.

Indulge your senses and attend a ballet production, a dramatic stage play, or a musical comedy and see why the artfully choreographed shows get such rave reviews.

1212 E. 45th Pl., Tulsa, OK 74105
(918) 749-6030, www.tulsaballet.org

DECOPOLIS
LIS
TOYS
Ice Cream!

SHOPPING AND FASHION

95

FIND EVERYTHING TULSA
AT THESE LOCAL SHOPS

In the heart of downtown Tulsa, you will find some of our best shopping treasures. The stores called Decopolis, Ida Red, Buck Atoms Cosmic Curios, and Boomtown Tees offer you everything you need be a true Tulsan. They deliver serious retro-inspired gifts, toys, and merchandise. You can find an abundance of unique books, clothing, Tulsa-made items, souvenirs, gifts, cards, and more that will keep you entertained for hours, and each place provides different hard-to-find novelty items. When looking for a special gift or Tulsa treasure, you can't go wrong with any of these gems.

Each of these local shops provides a different angle on love for our local culture. Decopolis is an homage to the art deco glory days of Tulsa, and Buck Atoms Cosmic Curios celebrates retro kids' TV by mashing up cowboys with the space age and everything else weird and wonderful. Boomtown Tees offers apparel for the proud Okie, and Ida Red, "Oklahoma's General Store," is all about locally made fun and funky items. Ida Red has a Brookside location in addition to its downtown storefront. With all these options, you are sure to find that special someone the perfect gift.

Decopolis
502 S. Boston Ave., Tulsa, OK 74103
(918) 382-7388, www.decopolis.net

Ida Red
208 N. Main St., Tulsa, OK 74103
(918) 398-6700, www.idaredgeneralstore.com

Buck Atoms Cosmic Curios on 66
1347 E. 11th St., Tulsa, OK 74120
www.buckatomson66.com

Boomtown Tees
114-A S. Elgin Ave., Tulsa, OK 74120
(918) 938-6000, www.boomtowntees.com

HONE YOUR GIFT-HUNTING SKILLS
AT THE SHOPPING MALLS

Tulsa has Woodland Hills Mall, Tulsa Hills Shopping Center, Utica Square, Southroads, and The Farm and Fontana Shopping Centers, just to name a few.

There are many other shopping strips around Tulsa as well. The Kingspointe shopping center at 61st and Yale offers a variety of eateries and places to shop and play. There is a little strip mall at 31st and Harvard that has several eclectic shops where you can find a perfect gift. Places like The Shops of Seville and Utica Square can help you locate special upscale finds and treasures.

Tulsa has no shortage of exclusive shops and boutiques, and a few of them can be found along Boston Avenue or in the Pearl, Arts, or Deco Districts. However, southern and central Tulsa have a variety of specialty shops that offer distinctive finds as well. Little shops like The Perfect Touch at 91st and Yale and Kiddlestix Toy Store at 41st and Harvard are just a few of the hidden treasures in Tulsa where you can find more than you thought you were looking for.

In the near future, a new outlet mall will go up near Jenks, area so there will be even more shopping pleasures ahead!

Woodland Hills Mall
7021 S. Memorial Dr., Tulsa, OK 74133

The Farm Shopping Center
5321 S. Sheridan Rd., Tulsa, OK 74145

Southroads Mall
5211 E. 41st St., Tulsa, OK 74136

Shops of Seville
10051 S. Yale Ave., Tulsa, OK 74137

Utica Square
2070 Utica Square, Tulsa, OK 74114

Tulsa Hills Shopping Center
7380 S. Olympia Ave., Tulsa, OK 74132

Kingspointe Village Shopping Center
5984 S. Yale Ave., Tulsa, OK 74135

Fontana Shopping Center
7837 E. 51st St., Tulsa, OK 74145

The Vineyard On Memorial
7890 E. 106th Pl. S., Tulsa, OK 74133

97

FIND YOUR SPECIAL TREASURE
AT THE TULSA FLEA MARKET

For nearly fifty years, Tulsans and visitors have found special treasures at the Tulsa Flea Market. Located in Expo Square at 21st Street and Yale Avenue, this long-standing Tulsa tradition is the place to go to find rare, unique, or vintage clothing, shoes, antiques, books, and more. This flea market is family owned and operated and purports to be a "different kind of flea market."

Everything from collectibles to memorabilia is offered by vendors from the tri-state area and beyond. You can find booth after booth of special treasures in over fifty thousand square feet of merchandise, so you may want to set aside an entire day for browsing through the nostalgic trinkets of yesteryear.

Pets are welcome, concessions are available, and the flea market is open most Saturdays from 8:00 a.m. until 4:00 p.m. The market is held indoors, which is great for the unpredictable Tulsa weather and admission is free to the public. The schedule changes at certain times of the year, so it's best to check their website and schedule to be sure the flea market is open.

4145 E. 21st St., Tulsa, OK 74114
www.tulsafleamarket.net/index.html

98

SPARK YOUR INNER ELEGANCE AT UTICA SQUARE

Opened in 1952 as Tulsa's first suburban shopping center, Utica Square has become a Tulsa tradition that is elegant and meticulously planned.

Eclectic events from free concerts to sophisticated light displays at Christmastime make this an entertainment center where buying things seems like a perk. It is the one place in Tulsa where gift hunters can find upscale specialty stores like Saks Fifth Avenue, Williams-Sonoma, and Pottery Barn when looking for that important gift for a wedding or a special someone.

Artfully decorated pathways lined with delightful red telephone booths and large clocks add to Utica Square's charm. Over three hundred trees adorn the property, which successfully combines French Country and Georgian designs.

It is worth the trip to stroll through Utica Square if only to window shop in this comfortable and elegant setting.

1709 Utica Square, Tulsa, OK 74114
(918) 742-5531, www.uticasquare.com/

99

GO OFF THE BEATEN PATH
FOR DOWNTOWN BOUTIQUES

Downtown Tulsa comprises seven different districts. Each of them has its own distinctive place in the downtown collage and each offers a variety of one-of-a-kind boutiques, restaurants, specialty stores, and more.

Take a day to explore them all. You might be pleasantly surprised by the out-of-the-way treasures, and you will find to your delight that Tulsa is an entrepreneurial city full of artists, performers, and craftspeople who are all eager to share their talents.

In each district you will find specialty stores connected to the district's name. For example, in the Arts District, you will find art galleries and museums. In the Cathedral District you will find more churches and venues of spiritual interest. In the Deco District you will find places that celebrate the history of Tulsa's art deco past. Within each of them, you can find shops and artifacts peculiar to the district and items devoted specifically to the city of Tulsa.

If you will be here for a while, it's a good idea to take the time to explore all of the districts in Tulsa to discover each one's unique charm so you can go back again and again.

HOP ON THE BOXCAR TREND
AT BOXYARD

One of the most unique shopping destinations in Tulsa, found in the Greenwood District, is made up of shipping containers that have traveled all over the world. This retail hub was inspired by an iconic London development.

Large cargo boxes that were used for years to ship all kinds of products internationally are recommissioned to become mini-stores that sell things as unusual as the packing they come in. From eclectic to specific and everything in between, the Boxyard offers a variety of food, clothing, and signature drinks from local small businesses and entrepreneurs.

Fairly new to Tulsa, this clever idea is the brainchild of local developers who had a vision for a shopping experience like no other. With second-story open seating offering a beautiful view of downtown Tulsa, this quirky space provides something that no other shopping center offers and makes the Boxyard a special, interesting, and really fun place to shop and enjoy time with family and friends.

502 E. 3rd St., Tulsa, OK 74120
www.tulsaboxyard.com

CAINS
BALLROOM
DANCING

SUGGESTED ITINERARIES

GET OUTSIDE

TOURS AND MORE

EXPLORE!

DATE NIGHT

FAMILY FRIENDLY

GOOD EATIN'

IT'S ALL ABOUT TULSA

ACTIVITIES BY SEASON

SPRING

SUMMER

FALL

WINTER

INDEX